50 STRATEGIES for Supporting Multilingual Learners

Mandy Manning, M.A.

Consultant

Carla Tott, M.A., Bilingual Educator, Eagle Rock, California

Publishing Credits

Corinne Burton, M.A.Ed., *President* and *Publisher*
Aubrie Nielsen, M.S.Ed., *EVP of Content Development*
Kyra Ostendorf, M.Ed., *Publisher, professional books*
Véronique Bos, *VP of Creative*
Cathy Hernandez, *Senior Content Manager*
Kevin Pham, *Graphic Designer*

Image Credits

All images from iStock and/or Shutterstock

Library of Congress Cataloging-in-Publication Data
Names: Manning, Mandy R., author.
Title: 50 strategies for supporting multilingual learners / Mandy Manning.
Description: Huntington Beach, CA : Shell Educational Publishing, Inc., 2024. | Includes bibliographical references. | Summary: "50 actionable strategies for multilingual learner success in diverse classrooms, backed by robust research"-- Provided by publisher.
Identifiers: LCCN 2023059606 (print) | LCCN 2023059607 (ebook) | ISBN 9798765946244 (paperback) | ISBN 9798765946251 (ebook)
Subjects: LCSH: Multilingual education. | English language--Study and teaching--Foreign speakers. | Language acquisition. | BISAC: EDUCATION / Bilingual Education | EDUCATION / Teaching / Methods & Strategies
Classification: LCC LC3715 .M357 2024 (print) | LCC LC3715 (ebook) | DDC 370.117/5--dc23/eng/20240401
LC record available at https://lccn.loc.gov/2023059606
LC ebook record available at https://lccn.loc.gov/2023059607

A division of Teacher Created Materials
5482 Argosy Avenue
Huntington Beach, CA 92649
www.tcmpub.com/shell-education
ISBN 979-8-7659-4624-4

Printed by: **51307**
Printed In: **USA**
PO#: 11669

Table of Contents

Welcome

Being a teacher is a tremendous gift exchange. Not the exchange of physical things, but of what really matters in our lives—human connection and the gifts we receive when we share our cultures, our experiences, and our talents with one another to make our classroom communities places in which every student feels valued, welcome, and able to learn. At the heart of effective teaching are the connections we have with our students and our knowledge of who they are as learners and as individual human beings with a variety of strengths and dreams. Being open to who our students are helps us meet their needs, and in return, we gain so much.

Over the years in my classroom, I have had the privilege of meeting newcomers to our community. These students enriched our classroom through their cultures, languages, experiences, and perspectives. It was my honor to welcome them and help them transition to learning in a new environment and living in a new community.

Students remind us every day that each of them is an individual and that we must be open to connecting with them and finding out who they are, so we can effectively teach them. It is only through reaching across differences, embracing one another's diversity, and accepting one another as we are that we are stronger, safer, and more connected as a community.

My hope is that this book will help you connect with and support culturally and linguistically diverse students—and all students—in your classroom. These strategies come from my 21 years as a classroom teacher (most of which were spent teaching multilingual learners), collaborations with and learning from my colleagues, reading research, and pure trial and error. At the heart of each approach are connecting with students, building relationships, and teaching students the strategies for being independent, lifelong learners. Whether you have one multilingual learner or a whole classroom full, add these approaches to your practice and adapt them based on the needs of your students to make them your own.

—Mandy Manning
2018 National Teacher of the Year

Teaching Multilingual Learners

This book is designed to support you in your work with multilingual learners (MLs) by providing an overview of concepts of language acquisition and language proficiency, as well as foundational knowledge of how to support the MLs in your classroom. While many of the strategies in this book may be familiar, the key difference is in the inclusion of language learning and intentional scaffolding to support MLs in learning content while also learning content-related language.

I began my career in education as a paraeducator working with special education students, moved on to become an English language arts teacher, and eventually I became a full-time English language development specialist. Each of these experiences taught me that building relationships, creating community, and focusing on connection are paramount to ensuring every student has access to learning in the classroom. That is why this book begins with strategies for creating school and classroom environments where multilingual learners feel a sense of welcome and belonging. The remainder of the strategies are focused on language and content support for MLs. First you will find general language support strategies, followed by targeted strategies for the four domains of language: listening and speaking, reading, and writing. These are followed by strategies for developing visual literacy and implementing supportive assessment.

This resource begins with basic ideas related to multilingual learners. It is important to understand social versus academic language, the impact of the affective filter, the difference between English language acquisition and English language proficiency, the meaning of comprehensible input and output, and one key practice, enunciation. The foundational knowledge in this introduction will help frame how you serve and support your students.

Basic Interpersonal Communication Skills

Basic interpersonal communication skills (BICS) are the social language skills students use during face-to-face social interactions (Cummins 2008). These skills develop quickly. Students can become adept at social English anywhere from six months to two years after arriving in the United States. Social language is less demanding than academic language and is context embedded, meaning the language comes from a shared understanding of the topic of conversation. During these everyday conversations, gestures and facial expressions help create the meaning. When students have proficiency in BICS, educators may be misled into believing students have stronger academic English-language skills than they actually do.

Cognitive Academic Language Proficiency

Cognitive academic language proficiency (CALP) refers to the skills and knowledge students have in using content-related academic language (Cummins 2008). Students with CALP can function effectively in a classroom and are able to engage in language that is abstract and not always context embedded. They can engage in complex critical thinking, using advanced academic language. CALP takes longer to acquire than BICS, requiring up to five years to become proficient.

Stages of New Language Acquisition

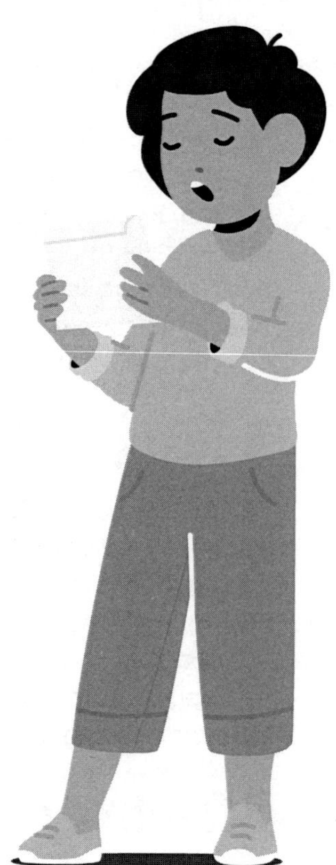

New language acquisition is the process by which learners acquire an additional language outside of their first language. This process includes learning the grammar, structures, and functions for oral and written language production. There are six stages of acquiring a new language (Robertson and Ford, n.d.). Learners move through each stage at their own pace depending on fluency and skills in their first language, prior formal education, academic skills, and individual learning differences. Stages of new language acquisition are not measured using a test; they are assessed formatively.

Pre-Production

During pre-production, students are learning receptive language. This is also known as the "silent period." Learners are receiving language through listening and reading but producing little to no oral or written language. This stage lasts six weeks or longer. Learners at this stage need the space to be silent and focus on familiarizing themselves with the new language.

Early Production

During early production, learners use single words and short phrases, and tend to make a lot of mistakes. Their responses are brief, and they struggle with conversation. They are still working heavily on their receptive language skills. Continue to be patient with students in early production, supporting them in vocabulary development and in learning words and phrases in context, while allowing them this relatively quiet period in their development.

Speech Emergent

When learners become speech emergent, they use more complex sentences and can have longer conversations. They are most successful with social language and language used in context. These learners are acquiring more vocabulary and making fewer mistakes. They are gaining confidence. At this stage it is important to be supportive and to avoid overcorrecting mistakes.

Beginning Fluency

Learners at the beginning fluency stage are adept at social communication. They appear to have strong receptive and productive skills. However, students are still acquiring academic language skills and continue to struggle with producing language in new contexts with unfamiliar vocabulary and language structures. This is a tricky stage as it can appear that students have more ability than they do because they so easily communicate with their peers. It is important to continue to support students as they acquire academic language skills.

Intermediate Fluency

Learners with intermediate fluency converse easily socially and are nearing fluency in academic contexts. They still have gaps when learning new academic vocabulary and language structures but with support make few mistakes. At this stage learners can share their opinions and engage in argumentation. With basic support such as graphic organizers, students can access learning in general education classrooms and should be challenged to engage in analysis and synthesis of information.

Advanced Fluency

Learners at this stage have native-like fluency in the new language. They can engage in social and academic contexts with ease and are adept at learning new information in the new language. They may have an accent and make mistakes with culture-specific language, such as idioms. Otherwise, they speak English comfortably and are fully literate. These learners have usually exited out of English language support services as they do not need support beyond that provided for students who speak English as their first language.

Affective Filter

The affective filter (Krashen and Terrell 1983) is thought of as an internal monitor, somewhat like an editor or critic, which can impede multilingual learners' willingness to take risks or produce language, as they fear they will make mistakes. The affective filter can impact motivation and confidence, and it causes anxiety, which then becomes a barrier to learning. As a teacher, it is essential to provide a supportive learning environment with the supports and scaffolds students need so their affective filters are lowered and they can acquire the new language.

Levels of English Language Proficiency

While English language proficiency levels and the stages of new language acquisition align, they are not the same. English language proficiency refers to the level of academic language knowledge and skill at which students are performing. Language proficiency is measured using standardized assessments. Each student's score provides insight as to the level of language they can process, understand, produce, and use. Language proficiency levels inform accommodations for each student. WIDA (World-class Instructional Design and Assessment) offers the ACCESS collection of assessments, but there are several other options. The following are the six levels outlined in the WIDA standards (2007). These standards may differ slightly from those used in your district.

Level 1 Entering

Students at level 1 have limited to no English language proficiency. They have limited to no understanding of spoken English, generally cannot speak English, and are not literate in English. Teaching level 1 students should include using visuals to support comprehension, keeping instructions short, allowing for short-answer responses, focusing on foundational language skills, and incorporating movement and nonverbal responses, such as drawing.

Level 2 Beginning

Students at level 2 have limited English language proficiency and are beginning to gain academic language skills. They increasingly understand more language than they can produce. These students make many errors and their productive language, whether oral or written, is difficult to understand. They use short sentences and basic language structures. Teaching level 2 students should continue to include providing visual support, keeping instructions short while adding more academic language, allowing short-answer responses while encouraging the use of content-related language, continuing to incorporate movement during instruction, and providing structured support to help students produce academic language structures.

Level 3 Developing

Students at level 3 are increasing their understanding of content-related academic language. They are producing more language and are able to use longer sentences and write short paragraphs. Students continue to make mistakes, but these are fewer and fewer, and the written and oral language they produce is increasingly easy to understand. Teaching level 3 students should continue to include visual support for content. Begin introducing increasingly complex language structures and pushing students to provide longer responses both orally and in writing. Social language will increase rapidly at this level and students will use slang. Encourage them to use academic language during class.

Level 4 Expanding

Students at level 4 can connect complex topics and understand academic language in context. They are producing content-related language more accurately and can write multiple paragraphs and connect topics, moving from one topic to the other with increasing ease. Teaching students at level 4 should include more sophisticated visual supports and intentional instruction in visual literacy to ensure students know how to use texts and other support materials in their learning. Provide students with support in organizing and structuring their ideas.

Level 5 Bridging

Students at level 5 are nearing the same level of academic language fluency as their peers whose first language is English. They can produce written and oral content-related language using a variety of sentences and paragraph lengths. They are writing essays, longer narratives, and in-depth projects. Teaching level 5 students is similar to teaching students whose first language is English. Continue to provide structured support when asking students to complete complex assignments, projects, or writing.

Level 6 Reaching

Students at level 6 are essentially fluent and literate in social and academic language. They can function at the same level as their peers whose first language is English. Teaching level 6 students is the same as teaching students whose first language is English. Provide additional assistance in transitioning to full independence without English language development support.

Comprehensible Input and Output

For multilingual students to learn content and acquire content language, instruction must be comprehensible. *Comprehensible input* refers to the instructional level at which multilingual learners can acquire language (Krashen 1981). Students learn when instruction is slightly above their current level of proficiency. Therefore, it is essential to consider the language proficiency levels of your students and use that information to plan instruction and develop supports to ensure students can access learning and be successful.

Consideration must also be given to the language outputs of multilingual students when acquiring new language. *Comprehensible output* hypothesizes that learning occurs when multilingual learners learn from mistakes they make when using the new language (Swain 2005). When students engage their mental processing to recognize gaps in their language output between what they want to say versus what they are able to say based on their current knowledge, learn from their mistakes, and adjust based on those mistakes, language acquisition occurs. Support multilingual learners in viewing mistakes as an important step toward language proficiency.

The Importance of Enunciation

As you begin to use the strategies in this book, keep in mind the importance of enunciation. While this may seem obvious, enunciating is easier said than done when teaching. As proficient speakers of English, we tend to speak quickly and connect our words together, making it difficult for multilingual learners to understand what we are saying. It is crucial to adjust our speed, speak clearly, and enunciate every word when teaching multilingual learners. Remember, it is also critical for multilingual learners to hear and understand English in different accents. When students hear and can understand English in a variety of accents, they are empowered and gain confidence when they speak. So enunciation does not mean accents should be diminished. Enunciation refers to ensuring words are clear and understandable for multilingual learners.

Tips for PK–1

- Lessons tend to be high energy and fast-paced, which can make enunciation difficult. Even when an activity is fast-paced, it is important to speak clearly at a normal speed.
- When using songs for instruction, every word should be clearly enunciated. Model the song and ensure students can hear each individual word.
- When reading aloud to the class, reduce your speed just slightly, enunciate, and use inflection to model dialogue.

Tips for Grades 2–5

- Enunciation is essential when teaching new skills and concepts that students must master and build on as they move through school.
- In addition to ensuring you are speaking at a normal rate of speed, not too fast and not too slow, and speaking clearly, it is important to ensure students are also speaking clearly. When students speak and their language is not clear, repeat what they say—not as a correction but as a model so all students can understand what their classmates have said.

Tips for Grades 6–12

- Subject-area classes have advanced vocabulary that often is not spelled the way it sounds and contains many syllables. Model this language for students, clearly enunciating each part of a word.
- Instructions and texts are more complex. Clearly enunciate when you are giving directions and when reading complex texts aloud. Ensure there is enough space between words so they do not run together.

Tips for All Levels

- Tap into students' prior knowledge during instruction. Multilingual learners often have significant content knowledge, but simply do not yet have the English language skills to articulate that knowledge. Honor students' prior knowledge and skills and help them use academic English language to demonstrate their knowledge. When learning a new language, multilingual learners must learn how to code switch, translate, and retranslate in their heads. Guide, practice, and nurture these skills.
- When showing videos, use subtitles. Movies, shows, and video clips can be very difficult to understand due to soundtracks and scores, accents, and fast-paced dialogue.
- When giving directions, writing them as you speak can ensure that you enunciate, as the process of writing slows down your speaking.
- Avoid using a condescending tone or increasing your volume. When speaking with multilingual learners, people often drop articles, such as "the," especially when speaking with newcomers. Be conscious of this and ensure you always use correct grammar to model language.

How to Use This Book

Choose a strategy and give it a try! Most activities use common items found in schools and classrooms, but there are some where you'll likely need to gather additional materials.

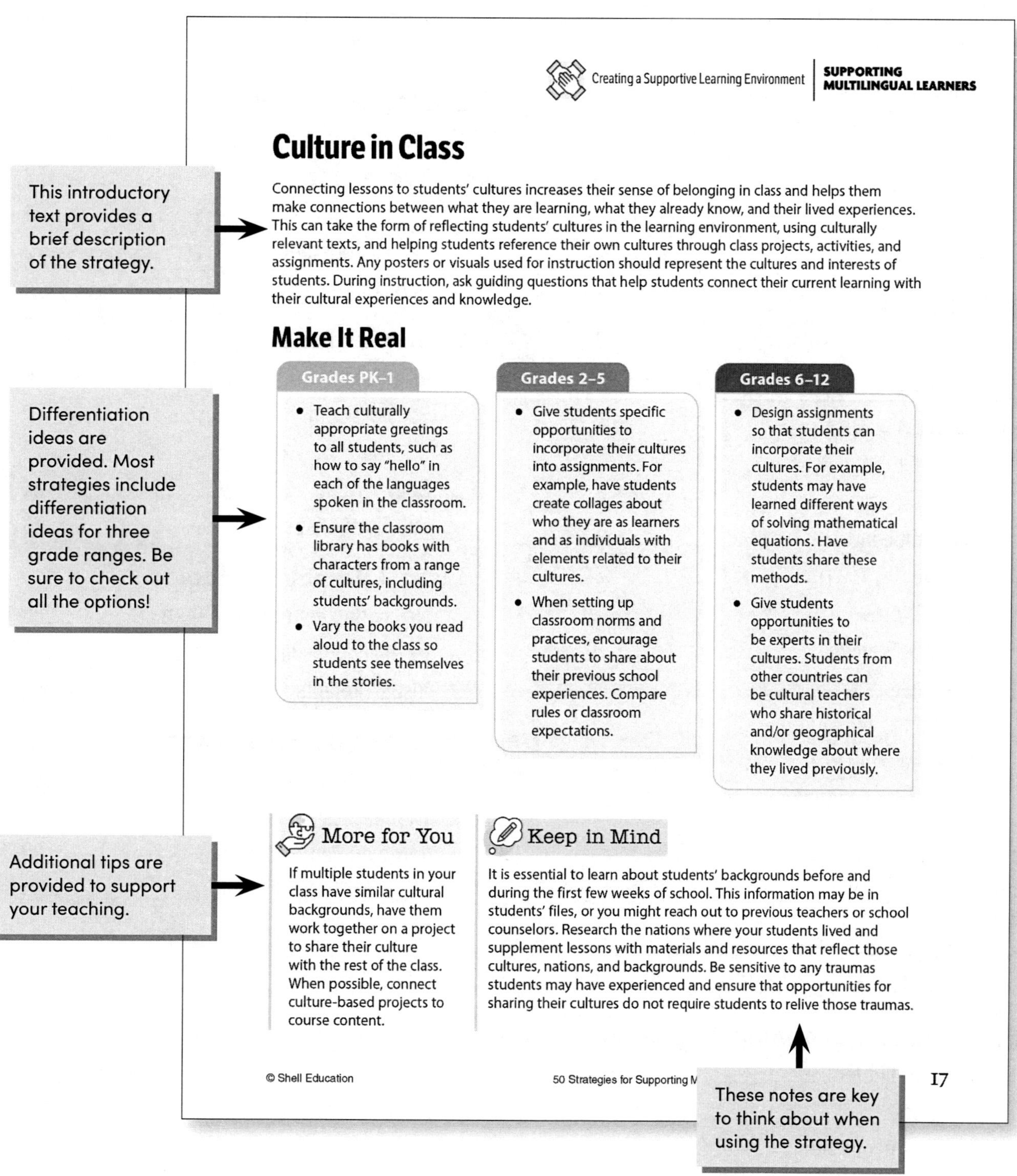

Strategies Table of Contents

Creating a Supportive Learning Environment

General Language Support Strategies

Strategies for Listening & Speaking

Strategies for Reading

Strategies for Writing

Visual Literacy Strategies

Supportive Assessment

Focus on Community

Building community in your classroom is critical to reaching and teaching multilingual learners. Students need to feel valued by and connected with their teacher and their peers to be comfortable using new language and taking academic risks. Spend the first few weeks of school focused on building a strong classroom community.

Make It Real

Grades PK–1

- Ask students to create art that shares something about themselves. This can be structured as a show and tell. Have students draw pictures of the things they like or complete a similar project. Help them introduce themselves to one another, offering multiple avenues so that students at all language levels may participate—keep in mind some students may not yet be able to introduce themselves in English.
- Have students play games through which they connect and learn to work cooperatively. For example, the game "In the Middle" helps students find similarities with their peers. Students stand in a circle, and the teacher calls out a characteristic, such as "brown eyes," and all students who have brown eyes go to the middle.
- Quick check-ins are best when students are engaged in unstructured activities, such as snack time, playtime, or other breaks. Being present during unstructured time will also help identify if MLs are connecting socially with their peers.

Grades 2–5

In addition to academic skills, these students are learning how to navigate interpersonal relationships.

- Assign students a get-to-know-you project to share their interests and who they are outside of school. This can be a brown-bag speech, a poster about themselves, or some other "I am" project.
- Provide opportunities for students to discuss differences productively, with curiosity rather than judgment. Use whole-group discussion when there is an issue the whole class needs to resolve. Facilitate one-to-one conversations to help students learn how to have difficult conversations that lead to repaired relationships.
- Social opportunities are critical. Periodically incorporate social activities that intentionally promote positive interactions between students, such as playing board games or having a discussion using social prompts.

Continued

Grades 6–12

For many students at this level, opportunities to build community may be limited, so being intentional is especially important.

- Develop community systems such as regular class meetings, established times for checking in, and scheduled team-building or social activities.
- Assign a get-to-know-you project. If students are reluctant to present to the class, do a gallery walk and then have students pair up and ask one another questions based on what they learned from seeing the projects.
- Social opportunities can be used for conversation practice. Set aside a few minutes each week to give students a social topic such as "music you enjoy listening to," and have them discuss the topic with their neighbors.
- Schedule regular one-to-one time with students to check on their academic progress, but more importantly to make sure they are feeling confident and secure and to allow them time to share anything happening in their lives that might impact their performance in class

More for You

Conducting classroom circles (or classroom meetings) is one way to build community. This is especially true for MLs, as circles can be used as a cultural bridge to help students navigate learning within new classroom and cultural environments. Classroom circles can be conducted daily, weekly, or periodically. Use them for getting to know one another at the start of the day, to process learning, to set the schedule for the day or week, to review and decompress, and to work through difficulties as a class and solve problems together. Classroom circles are common in elementary school. They can be an effective strategy at the secondary level to give students time to share and socialize, which helps students be more ready to learn.

Keep in Mind

Continue using community-building activities throughout the year. In addition to creating connections among students, find opportunities to connect with students one-to-one. Participate in social activities, and check in with students when they are working in groups or independently.

Culture in Class

Connecting lessons to students' cultures increases their sense of belonging in class and helps them make connections between what they are learning, what they already know, and their lived experiences. This can take the form of reflecting students' cultures in the learning environment, using culturally relevant texts, and helping students reference their own cultures through class projects, activities, and assignments. Any posters or visuals used for instruction should represent the cultures and interests of students. During instruction, ask guiding questions that help students connect their current learning with their cultural experiences and knowledge.

Make It Real

Grades PK–1

- Teach culturally appropriate greetings to all students, such as how to say "hello" in each of the languages spoken in the classroom.
- Ensure the classroom library has books with characters from a range of cultures, including students' backgrounds.
- Vary the books you read aloud to the class so students see themselves in the stories.

Grades 2–5

- Give students specific opportunities to incorporate their cultures into assignments. For example, have students create collages about who they are as learners and as individuals with elements related to their cultures.
- When setting up classroom norms and practices, encourage students to share about their previous school experiences. Compare rules or classroom expectations.

Grades 6–12

- Design assignments so that students can incorporate their cultures. For example, students may have learned different ways of solving mathematical equations. Have students share these methods.
- Give students opportunities to be experts in their cultures. Students from other countries can be cultural teachers who share historical and/or geographical knowledge about where they lived previously.

More for You

If multiple students in your class have similar cultural backgrounds, have them work together on a project to share their culture with the rest of the class. When possible, connect culture-based projects to course content.

Keep in Mind

It is essential to learn about students' backgrounds before and during the first few weeks of school. This information may be in students' files, or you might reach out to previous teachers or school counselors. Research the nations where your students lived and supplement lessons with materials and resources that reflect those cultures, nations, and backgrounds. Be sensitive to any traumas students may have experienced and ensure that opportunities for sharing their cultures do not require students to relive those traumas.

Connect with Families

Connecting and building relationships with families is an important aspect of creating a supportive environment. The traditional means through which schools connect with families, such as back-to-school nights, may be inaccessible for culturally and linguistically diverse (CLD) families. To support family connections, consider providing transportation to and from school events, interpreter services in all languages spoken in your school community, and alternative times for individual conferences or meetings should families be unable to attend the community event. Communicate every connection opportunity in the families' languages.

Make It Real

Grades PK–1

Including parent volunteers in the classroom is a common practice in PK–1.

- Offer a wide variety of opportunities that do not require the volunteer to speak English. Volunteers can help organize the learning environment, chaperone field trips, help supervise recess, and support classroom activities.
- Ensure that all communications about volunteer opportunities are provided in the languages spoken by your students' families.
- During beginning-of-the-year conferences, schedule CLD families first so that interpreters can be reserved well in advance. Encourage the school district to schedule events on different nights so interpreters are not overloaded and services can be provided to all families.

Grades 2–5

In addition to making volunteer opportunities accessible, encourage families to support learning through their cultural knowledge.

- Invite families to participate in classroom projects. For example, when teaching about countries in social studies, reach out to families who have roots in those countries to talk about or introduce different aspects of their cultures. They can demonstrate a craft or share other cultural elements.
- The early grades are a good opportunity to begin introducing families to ways they can support their students at home with their learning. Provide flexible opportunities for families to learn about what is being taught and specific strategies they can use to support their children.

Grades 6–12

Contact with families in the upper grades is heavily connected to academics. Provide information about how parents can partner with the school to support student success.

- CLD families may need assistance in navigating school systems that help them support their children. Provide multiple opportunities throughout the year to help families check their children's academic progress. Provide guidance for parents on supporting their children with homework reminders and on creating structures at home that will help students achieve their academic goals.
- When planning parent-teacher conferences, provide flexible meeting times during which you can meet with the families of your MLs. Ensure there are interpreters available.

More for You

Conducting informal home visits can be an effective way to begin forming relationships with your students' families. The visits provide insight into their home lives, their family structures, and their cultures (El Yaafouri 2017). Follow your district or school guidelines when planning home visits. Initial visits should be informal with the aim of meeting and getting to know one another. Home visits can be followed up with more formal student-parent-teacher conferences at school with interpretation services, if needed.

Keep in Mind

Schools often schedule multicultural events to connect to the diverse families in their communities. Plan and implement these events so that all families can participate without unfair financial impact. Arrange for adult interpreters, optimally professionals, when meeting with families. Avoid having children interpret for their parents during parent-teacher conferences; this impacts family power dynamics and can lead to dishonesty and distrust.

Foster Connections for Language Practice

Students need authentic opportunities to practice language. Connecting multilingual learners with English-speaking peers to engage in natural dialogue helps improve their productive and receptive language skills. Students become more comfortable listening to, understanding, and speaking English, and gain confidence and feel more connected to their school community. Connections can be made between classrooms, within culture and language groups, and between higher and lower grade levels, and they can be social or academic. Social connections should focus within the same grade or age span. Plan activities such as playing sports or board games, or sharing meals, to help students practice social language. Academic connections can cross grade levels. These connections focus on practicing the academic language students need for specific academic topics or units. Consider using technology to foster connections with classrooms in other schools or communities.

Make It Real

Grades PK–1

- For social connections, target specific interactions that will help MLs learn social language and culture in their new learning environment. Support students in learning how to interact in social environments, such as on the playground, and in learning the rules for schoolyard or classroom games.
- For academic connections, connect with a higher grade-level class. Students can be reading buddies, practice basic conversation, or make other content-based connections.

Grades 2–5

- Target specific social language skills such as making introductions and asking basic questions to learn about new friends.
- For academic language, connect with other classes at your school. Students at the same grade level can review or process learning to practice language. Older students can support younger students in their learning.
- Consider connecting your students with a high school class. The high school students can serve as mentors for your students. This helps students see older MLs being successful in the upper grades, giving them a vision for their own progress in the future.

Grades 6–12

- Help students who are new English learners connect with their native-English-speaking peers. Provide opportunities for these students to begin making friends with students outside of class time. Organize lunch basketball or lunchtime conversation partners.
- Partner with another class for cross-curricular learning connections. Develop shared projects to help students practice target academic language and learn the language for collaboration.
- To help students feel more confident in their interactions, provide conversation supports such as sentence starters or target vocabulary.

More for You

Use video conferencing software to facilitate connections with students in other schools, communities, or even countries. Bring in experts virtually to foster connections with your students.

There are websites that help teachers foster connections; for example, empatico.org, which is geared toward the elementary grades, and globalteacherprize.org/clubs, which connects teachers and classrooms globally.

Keep in Mind

Fostering connections must be intentional. Plan opportunities for social connections and connections embedded within learning both inside and outside of the classroom. Depending on language proficiency levels, older students may need support in social interactions. At upper grade levels, MLs often have a higher affective filter during social interactions. Make sure to provide sentence starters and fully prepare students prior to introducing them to new social situations.

Friends Helping Friends

Peer support is critical when teaching multilingual learners. There are several ways students can support one another. Peers can provide targeted feedback. They can provide first-language support when explaining new concepts or processing learning. Students can work in leveled groups (same level or high/low groupings) to support one another.

Make It Real

Grades PK–1

Peer support for younger children is social and academic.

- Have students work together in pairs to complete projects or activities.
- Before asking students to do independent work, have them practice in pairs or groups.
- When possible, allow students to socialize in their home languages with like-language peers.

Grades 2–5

Peer support should be targeted and prescribed for specific goals.

- Students can read in pairs, quiz one another, and use prompts to practice their learning.
- Assign roles in group work to ensure each member is responsible for a task that is appropriate for their language level.
- Model how to help, to ensure students understand the difference between helping their peer and giving the answers.

Grades 6–12

Peer support and collaboration is effective in helping students process and practice language.

- Use peer editing for specific purposes. Assign peer editing roles, with each student responsible for looking for specific errors.
- Conversation partners or small groups can be used for practicing target language, to review content, and to discuss learning.
- Allow students to work in their language groups to process learning in their home languages.

More for You

Give clear instructions for how to provide peer support along with the end goal for each peer support session. For example, if the goal is targeted feedback, assign roles detailing which partner does what during the session (e.g., who will give feedback and who will receive the feedback). Provide a detailed checklist of what the peer supporter should listen for, and provide instruction on how to receive feedback and how to ask clarifying questions. Before having students do a peer support session, model expectations by role-playing. Repeat this process any time there is a new expectation for a support session. It is essential to have structures in place so students know when and how to offer peer support.

Keep in Mind

In mixed-level groupings, ensure that higher-level students are still being challenged. Structure peer support so higher-level students can support their lower-level peers while also having the time and opportunity to expand their own learning.

The Bullet Point

Students benefit from being taught how to navigate directions, especially ones that are multi-step. Help students understand the expectations by writing each step as you give instructions. Providing a bulleted list instead of a paragraph is also helpful. Use only the language that is needed to convey the requirements of the assignment or activity, to make the directions accessible and easy to follow.

Make It Real

Grades PK–1

Including visual support for all written directions provides comprehensible input and supports students in understanding expectations.

- Provide visuals in the form of drawings, images, realia, or modeling along with written directions.
- Limit written directions to simple phrases as much as possible.
- Provide visuals and/or modeling for each step of the instructions.

Grades 2–5

Instructions should be modeled and written for students to follow.

- Provide both oral and written directions—as you say each step, write it on the board where all students can see it.
- Have students write the instructions themselves instead of giving them printed copies.
- Provide completed examples for students to reference as they complete assignments, activities, and projects. If these can be modeled or created as a group, that is most beneficial.

Grades 6–12

Often in these grades, instructions are provided in the form of paragraphs. Students need to be prepared to navigate these paragraphs.

- Model the process for students.
- Teach students how to break paragraphs into incremental steps and create their own bulleted lists.
- Have students rephrase what is expected to ensure they understand.
- Break instructions for longer projects into parts, providing directions for each part as students progress.

More for You

Providing bulleted or numbered lists of instructions helps students develop executive function. The visual of the list supports mental processing and working memory, and it helps students be organized and self-directed.

Keep in Mind

Multilingual learners have a heavier cognitive processing load than their English-speaking peers. Often students must translate what they are hearing or reading into their first language, and then translate again from the first language into English to write or speak. Providing short, digestible instructions that are numbered or bulleted eases this process, as students do not have to hold all of the steps in their heads while they are working through each individual step.

Continued

Examples

Grades PK–1 example

Draw 3 fruits.

- 1 red fruit
- 1 green fruit
- 1 yellow fruit

Grades 2–5 example

Write a paragraph about the phases of the moon.

Include:

- A topic sentence
- Three supporting details
- A closing sentence
- Capital letters and periods

Grades 6–12 example

Fill in the template to write the essay.

- Use the notes from the texts to explain the causes of the French Revolution.
- Give the information from the texts. Explain what this information means in your own words and why the information is important.
- Write a conclusion to explain the impact of the French Revolution. What were the results? What happened after it was over? How did this change history?
- Use transition words (for example, first, second, also, last, finally).
- Start your essay with an opening sentence, explaining what the essay is about.

Class Calendar

Support multilingual learners as they navigate structures and expectations of learning in a new culture while also learning English. Keep a class calendar to help students be organized, with special consideration for structures that may be new to MLs, such as homework or unit due dates, when to review for tests, school events like dress-up days, and so on. Build the calendar together and maintain it as a class. In addition, provide personal calendars or agendas for students to keep in their folders or notebooks.

Make It Real

Grades PK–1

Display a class calendar and engage students in adding items to it.

- Record class and school events on the calendar. Have students help with marking each day and each activity.
- Teach students the language of using a calendar. Use "repeat after me" to introduce new language, preview what will happen in class, and review language they have already learned.
- Incorporate daily language goals and revisit the calendar at the end of the day to mark off what the class accomplished.

Grades 2–5

Display a class calendar and teach students to maintain their own calendars.

- Include content topics in the calendar, and have students record the topics and assignments on their individual calendars or agendas. For each unit, determine the target language and have students write the language goal on the calendar.
- Have students use their personal calendars for content review and language practice at home. They can review their assignments and what they are learning and have a parent sign the calendar.
- To ensure calendaring does not take up too much class time, spend extra time at the start of the school year teaching how to use and maintain the class calendar, then make it a regular part of the class day, spending a few minutes at the start of each lesson adding to the calendar and double-checking it at the end of the day or close of the week. Add extra time at the end of a unit for students to revisit their unit language goals and mark their progress.

Continued

Grades 6–12

Maintain a class calendar (electronically, if possible) and check to make sure students are maintaining their own.

- Students can be responsible for updating the class calendar. Each time a new goal, assignment, project, or activity is planned, have students add it to the class and their individual calendars.
- Use the calendar to help MLs understand the pace of the school year, adding dates for progress reports, the end of the semester, school holidays, and so on.
- Teach students how to track progress (content and language) and plan using their personal calendars. Allow time at the beginning of the week to set up the calendar and at the close to check progress and review what students need to practice over the weekend.
- During independent work time, check in with individual students to see if they are using their calendars. Have students reflect on how the calendar helps them stay organized.

More for You

Effective use of an agenda or personal calendar is essential to improving executive functioning and becoming an independent learner. Executive function refers to our abilities to hold information in our brains through working memory, organizational abilities, and tracking progress and making goals (Zelazo, Blair, and Willoughby 2016). Students who have executive functioning skills have higher academic outcomes.

Keep in Mind

Calendaring helps MLs ask questions and articulate what they have been and are learning. Additionally, calendars are useful when students are reviewing content, as they can look back over the calendar and see reminders of what they have learned and what they should review for assessments.

Mile Markers

Establishing long-term goals for content-related language is essential to setting the direction learning must take for multilingual learners. Setting small goals or steps helps learners understand them and increases their likelihood of reaching the larger goals. It is easier to track student progress when the steps are clear and measurable, and such goals support reteaching in small pieces rather than needing to reteach an entire unit. Language goals should be focused on the vocabulary and sentence structures related to the content.

Make It Real

Grades PK–1

- Set daily content and language goals for students to help them focus and feel excited about their progress.
- Tell students the daily goal and have them repeat it.
- Help students track their progress and identify when they achieve a goal.
- Example: The content goal is to add single-digit numbers. The language goals focus on vocabulary students will use, such as *add* and *plus*, the phrase "put together," and sentence structures such as "5 plus 5 equals 10."

Grades 2–5

- Set daily and weekly goals for students. Have students write their weekly goal and then track the daily practice as they work toward it.
- Example: Students are learning how to write a persuasive argument. The content goal is to take a position and provide reasons for it. The language goals are based on the content goal. Set goals related to the language of writing, such as transition words, the sentence structures for using transition words, and writing a topic sentence.

Grades 6–12

- Set long-term goals with students; then set short-term goals that build toward the larger goal.
- Set daily goals at the start of class. Help students track their progress electronically or in writing. Teach students how to check their progress through the assessment system used by your district.
- Example: Students are learning about atoms. The content goal is to explain the three parts of an atom. The language goals are the vocabulary and sentence structures for describing these parts.

More for You

Beginning in upper elementary, incorporate technology into goal setting. Whatever districtwide technology programs students use should be utilized for goal setting, whether through a calendar program or other tracking options.

Keep in Mind

Every goal you set for students, or students set for themselves, must be achievable. It is also important to acknowledge every time a goal is met.

Celebrate Success

Celebrating success provides internal and external motivation and demonstrates to MLs that hard work is rewarded. Celebrate small and large successes based on individual and whole-class goals, and help students recognize and honor their own progress. Be clear as to why the class is receiving a reward, and when handing out individual rewards, reference the specific language and content goals students achieved. Goals must be achievable by the multilingual learners in your classroom, and it is essential to ensure they know how they contributed to the class reward.

Make It Real

Grades PK–1

Students in the early grades love celebrations. Even the smallest achievement should be celebrated. Help students celebrate individually and have class celebrations also.

- Track the progress of the whole class together. Make this a group endeavor, for example, by putting a marble in a jar each time students reach a personal goal. Choose a celebration, like "bring a stuffed animal day" or a special recess.
- Use small, tangible rewards for individual students, such as stickers and stamps.
- Example: A student goal may be to respond correctly when someone asks what their favorite color is. Once a student can do this accurately three times, they get to add a marble to the jar, and they get a sticker. When each student has at least one sticker, the whole class gets a reward.

Grades 2–5

Use whole-class celebrations to recognize when most of the class is making progress.

- Have students track their own progress toward goals. Rewards like fun pencils and special time with the teacher are effective.
- Track class progress with a point system. Set a point total for when the class gets to celebrate. Choose a celebration like a pajama and movie day or playing board games.
- Example: Students must read three independent reading books by set dates and write a paragraph summary of each book. Provide individual rewards for each book read and set a book total for the whole class, with a minimum of one book completed by each student. In this way, some students can read more than others, but all students contribute to the reward.

Grades 6–12

Goal achievement in the upper grades is not often celebrated, but it should be. Help students track their progress and create mile markers at which students are celebrated for their progress.

- Students need a way to track their own progress. If available, use technology. Students can create a goal, steps toward that goal, and a way to mark those steps. Have students notify you when they reach their goal.
- Students in the upper grades need larger rewards. Small gift cards and extra credit are good for this age group.
- Track whole-class progress. Let students know that when a certain percentage of the class reaches the goal, there will be a celebration. Choose a celebration like a pizza party or free time.

More for You

Allow students to carry their goals over to the next class day. Be flexible with timelines for achieving language and content goals. Consider utilizing a standards-based grading approach, which grades proficiency rather than tasks. Standards-based grading helps articulate what students know and are able to do and is based on determining proficiency in content and language goals (Link and Guskey 2022).

Keep in Mind

Goals for each student should be based on their language proficiency levels. For example, if students must write a fictional story with an inciting incident, rising action, climax, and denouement, some students may need to include only one action in their rising action, while others need three. All students must turn in a story to get the reward, but the definition of a "complete" story depends on each student's language level.

Step by Step

Teach skills and concepts step-by-step in small, digestible pieces. Chunking instruction into smaller pieces supports multilingual learners who are learning content and the related language simultaneously. During planning, determine the language components students need to master the content and demonstrate their understanding of it. Teach each element, including the vocabulary, sentence structures, and language outputs, building from one to the next. Often, vocabulary is taught at the start of the lesson. As new sentence structures are taught, pause, highlight the new language, and provide structured practice for using the language in the context of the content. Link previous learning to the current learning to create a through line for students, connecting content and connecting language to content. If necessary, access students' prior knowledge and review content from previous lessons before moving to the next component.

Make It Real

Grades PK–1

Intentional deconstruction of lessons into language and content is critical for young MLs to master the concepts.

- Introduce the overall topic of instruction, then teach it in steps. Begin with the vocabulary, followed by the sentence structures, and finally connect each of those into the larger concept.
- After teaching each element, give students an activity through which they can practice that element before moving onto the next.
- For example, when teaching students to identify colors, start with color words. Next teach students the sentence structures for describing the color of something. Then have students use the vocabulary and sentences. Each step should include language practice.

Grades 2–5

Students in these grades are learning increasingly complex skills and concepts that build toward larger concepts students must master.

- Think of lessons as building blocks. Determine the foundational knowledge and skills students need to get to the next level. Build one step on the next, toward the expected student output. Do this during planning and during instruction.
- For example, when teaching students to write a paragraph, break it into the parts of a paragraph: topic sentence, supporting details, and concluding sentence. Teach each element individually with an opportunity for students to practice each step, then combine them all into a single paragraph.

Grades 6–12

In secondary grades, learning becomes more complex with multiple components. Expected outputs are also more complex, including longer essays and projects requiring multiple elements.

- Instead of giving the instructions for a multi-step project all at once, explain the end goal, and then provide in-depth instructions for one part of the assignment at a time. Do not move on until students have completed the current step.
- Prior to moving to the next step, review the previous step and explicitly teach how that step and any previous steps connect to the next.
- At the conclusion of a project, provide the overall rubric and have students use it to determine if they have met all the required elements.

More for You

Use the ten plus two strategy during instruction for grades 4 and above. Provide direct instruction for no more than ten minutes, followed by at least two minutes of students actively engaging with the content being taught. Ten minutes is the limit for most students for receiving new information before they must engage with the new learning to comprehend and remember it (Let's TEACH 2016).

Keep in Mind

Helping students break down large projects or assignments into smaller pieces increases their confidence and their likelihood of success.

Examples

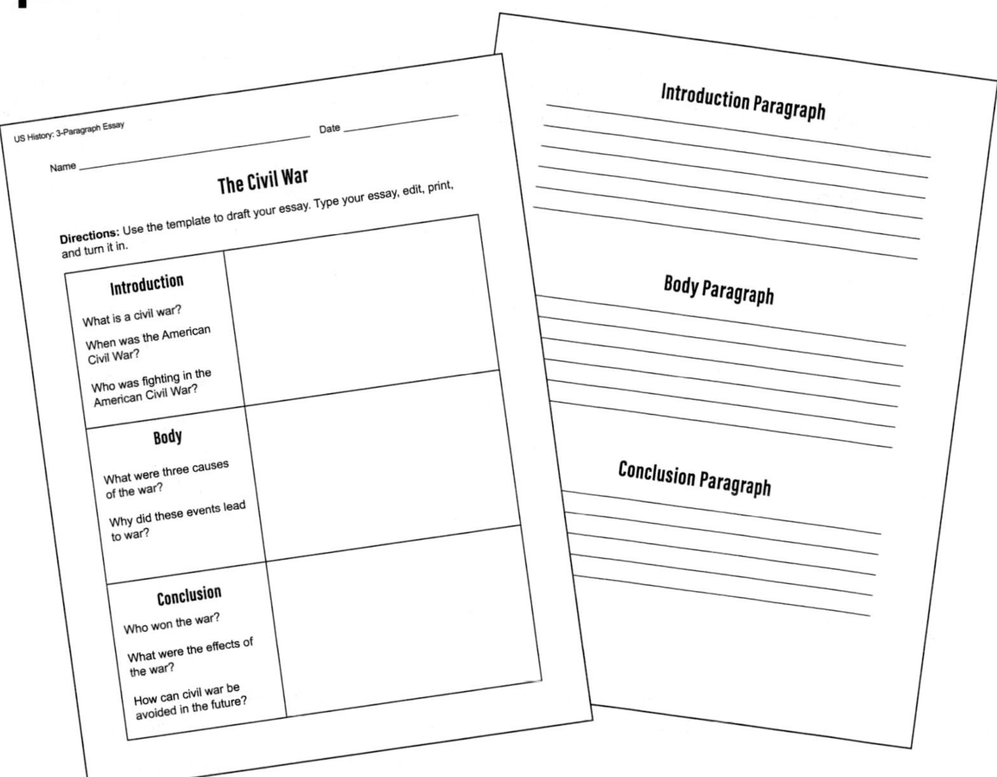

US History: 3-Paragraph Essay

Date

Name

The Civil War

Directions: Use the template to draft your essay. Type your essay, edit, print, and turn it in.

Introduction What is a civil war? When was the American Civil War? Who was fighting in the American Civil War?	
Body What were three causes of the war? Why did these events lead to war?	
Conclusion Who won the war? What were the effects of the war? How can civil war be avoided in the future?	

Introduction Paragraph

Body Paragraph

Conclusion Paragraph

Mini Lessons

Mini lessons are short moments of instruction (fewer than ten minutes) that provide context or instruction related to the larger lesson or unit. When multilingual learners are in our classrooms, it is essential to explicitly teach them language associated with the content. Mini lessons are a good option to address these language elements. Mini lessons can also be used in small groups as the teacher pulls MLs together to go over specific language elements. Teach mini lessons on the vocabulary, writing, or language structures students need to master content.

Make It Real

Grades PK–1

Students at this level have limited attention spans and need short teacher-led lessons. Mini lessons are a good fit for all content.

- Pre-teach or pause to teach any new vocabulary that arises. Do the same for any new sentence structures or questions.
- For young children, five minutes or fewer should suffice for a mini lesson, followed by an activity (song, choral response, and so on) to practice the new information.
- The mini-lesson can also be the activity—the song or choral response, without any formal introduction of the new language.

Grades 2–5

Ensuring MLs in these grades can understand every part of a lesson, especially the language elements, is critical.

- Focus on elements of language that students need to master the content. Teach new academic vocabulary as well as the related language structures.
- Word walls are effective. Add new vocabulary to the word wall. Refer students back to the word wall when the new language is repeated during a unit.
- Have students record new words on a graphic organizer that includes a picture of the word, the definition, and how it is used in context (within a sentence or a question).

Grades 6–12

Mini lessons at this level are asides incorporated into the overall lessons. Call out academic language or language structures, adding to the lesson rather than diverting focus from it.

- Take only a few minutes to point out academic language related to the new content. Do the same for any new sentence structures.
- Students can record new vocabulary and language structures in a graphic organizer or notebook. Have students keep these handy for reference.
- Review new vocabulary and language structures at the start and end of lessons or when the language is directly connected to part of a lesson.

Keep in Mind

Language becomes more complex and the need to know academic language increases as students move into the higher grades, regardless of their language proficiency levels. Explicitly teaching and reviewing academic vocabulary and language structures is critical for MLs to be successful.

Think Out Loud

Thinking out loud as you teach provides students with a model for language, as well as an example of problem-solving. Model correct pronunciation and intonation by processing learning aloud. As you process learning, demonstrate problem-solving strategies related to the content and navigating correct use of the language. When modeling how to think aloud for specific learning, post what you say, leaving blank lines students can fill in with what they are currently learning. Math and science are subjects in which think-alouds can be particularly useful.

Make It Real

Grades PK–1

- During the first weeks of school, use think-alouds to demonstrate how to meet, greet, make friends, and work through differences.
- Use think-alouds to process choosing words to use, how to structure sentences, how to spell words, and so on.
- Following instructions can also be modeled. For example, "I am drawing a picture of the main character. I need my pencil, my crayons, and a piece of paper." Take out each item as you talk. "If I'm not sure what I should do, I can look to see what other students are doing. Or, I can raise my hand and ask the teacher."

Grades 2–5

- As you model a new concept, think out loud about how previous learning informs your thinking about a new concept.
- When reading aloud, articulate how you connect what you are reading to what you have already read, or make comparisons to other texts or to current learning.
- Model academic processes. For example, "The first sentence talks about five students, so I should write down there are five students. The second sentence says they each need four markers. I should write that number and label too…" and so on.

Grades 6–12

- Use thinking out loud to connect language to complex academic content. Model for students how to formulate questions, solve problems, and structure answers.
- Encourage students to use thinking aloud in their own learning. Have students in small groups practice thinking out loud as they process and problem-solve together.
- For example, to demonstrate using a mind map to write an essay, say, "I have three topics on my mind map. Each of the topics has four details. I will use each topic for a new paragraph and the details as sentences in my paragraphs."

Keep in Mind

Academic thinking requires intention. The more intentional students can be in connecting prior learning to current learning, the best language to use and how to use it, and how to problem solve, the more successful they will be in school. Sharing how you process learning provides authentic examples for students.

I Do, We Do, You Do

Gradual release of responsibility is a common classroom practice (Frey and Fisher 2011). "I do, we do, you do" is even more critical when teaching multilingual learners. Model the language, task, or activity, then have students practice in groups or pairs. After students have seen what is expected of them and practiced together, they can attempt the work on their own.

Make It Real

Grades PK–1

Modeling language and expectations is critical for young learners.

- Students need to hear language pronounced and used correctly. Clearly use target language in context.
- Model expectations when giving directions. For instance, if you want students to match a color with the word for the color, show students several examples. Then have students practice as a whole class.
- Have students practice in pairs or groups. When possible, use groups with some MLs and some native speakers of English.
- Model basic directions. For example, take out an actual pencil as you tell students to take out a pencil.

Grades 2–5

Students are introduced to academic language with greater frequency.

- "I do, we do, you do" should be part of every lesson, especially when introducing a concept or setting an expectation for the first time.
- In addition to providing direct instruction on the language structures for a lesson, model how the language is used both orally and in writing.
- After whole-class practice such as choral repetition, answering questions as a class, or another type of participation, have students practice in pairs or groups.
- Monitor independent practice and reteach when necessary.

Grades 6–12

Because assignments and content are increasingly complex, "I do, we do, you do" is critical.

- Model oral language as well as written, giving added attention to language structures.
- Even in secondary grades, choral responses can be a low-risk way for students to practice language without feeling spotlighted.
- "I do, we do, you do" is essential when teaching writing. Students need explicit models they can follow when learning academic writing.
- Once students understand the expectations for writing, they can work in pairs or groups to write before writing on their own.

Keep in Mind

Multilingual learners who attended school in other countries may not understand U.S. classroom expectations. Model all school and classroom expectations and help students practice before expecting them to adhere to the norms and practices of your school community.

Guided Notes

During any activity in which students must listen to learn, providing notes that are already structured and partially completed helps students actively listen. Create an outline that has areas for students to fill in. This not only guides their listening, it highlights the most important information and provides a study guide. These note pages should be concise and target the content, academic language, and structures students are expected to understand and use. Guided notes are also good to help students gather information they need from texts or multimedia sources. The outline supports students in navigating the material and extracting the most essential information.

Make It Real

Grades PK–1

- After reading an informational text, introduce note-taking by developing an anchor chart together.
- Work with students to develop a list of important vocabulary words from the text.
- Display sentence frames with spaces for the vocabulary words students are learning. Fill in the "notes" together as a class.

Grades 2–5

- Support active listening by providing MLs with guided notes during reading, when learning new concepts, and while watching videos.
- Help students complete the guided notes while reading as a whole class and during lessons. Make sure all students have completed their guided notes correctly.
- Instruct students on how to use their notes to review their learning and prepare for assessments.

Grades 6–12

- Films and videos can be complicated for MLs to follow. Dialogue and narration are often fast-paced and difficult to understand. In addition to providing guided notes for students to use, it is beneficial to provide closed captioning.
- Offer students options for checking their notes to ensure they are filled out correctly. This can take the form of an answer key, working with a partner to compare notes, or a quick check by the teacher.

Continued

More for You

When using guided notes for reading, students can work in groups, with each group member responsible for completing the notes for a specific section. Group members can then share their notes with one another, so that all students have a complete set of notes at the end of the lesson. Giving students time to compare their notes ensures they are being responsible for their own learning and helps them recognize the importance of collaborative learning.

Keep in Mind

Note-taking is a skill that must be explicitly taught to all students. Listening with purpose, recognizing what constitutes essential information, and building good study habits by using notes are all part of being an independent learner. Guided notes are one strategy for supporting students in learning the skill of note-taking.

Example

Erosion

Erosion is the process by which ________ and ________ are gradually ________________ by environmental factors.

There are ________ types of erosion: water, wind, ice, and gravity.

1. ____________ erodes the land when water from rivers, creeks, or heavy rain ______________ the soil and rock, changing the ________ of the land.
2. ________ erodes the land by moving dirt ________, slowly removing layers of ________ from the land. This can impact how ________ the soil is for farming.
3. ________ erosion is caused by large ice masses, known as ________, slowly eroding the land when they move. Glaciers often make a ________ in the land.
4. ________ erosion occurs when the rock and soil ________________ due to gravity. ________________ are one type of gravity erosion.

Another cause of erosion is ________________. Humans cause erosion when they ________________, engage in ________________, and through ________________.

Sentence Frames

Provide students with sentence frames to support correct use of language and boost their confidence. A sentence frame provides part of a sentence with blanks for students to fill in. Students use sentence frames to ask or answer questions, to participate in discussions, or as prompts to begin writing or to develop writing. For example, during get-to-know-you discussions, social prompts provided orally or displayed in writing can include question frames such as "What is your favorite ______?" and answer frames such as "My favorite ______ is ______."

Make It Real

Grades PK–1

- Orally model phrasing students should use. Once they are familiar with it, use the phrase again, but pause and have students complete the sentence with their own information.
- This works well with greetings and descriptions. For example, to teach introductions, point to yourself and say, "I am Ms. Smith." Repeat three times. Follow this with a question, "What is your name?" Say the first part of the phrase, "I am," then point to the student and pause for them to fill in their name. Then repeat the process.
- Display written sentence frames even if students cannot yet read. This will help them learn to recognize words and will provide reinforcement when you reference the written frames during the lesson.

Grades 2–5

- Use sentence frames for everyday/social conversation and for academic discussions, vocabulary and language practice, and writing.
- During class discussions, provide frames students can use to ask questions and form responses. For example, if students are discussing a story they read, provide sentence frames to help them ask questions, such as, "Who was the main character of the story?" Also provide frames for the answers, such as, "The main character ______."
- Paragraph frames can be used when teaching writing genres. Provide students with a frame that helps them compose introductory sentences, supporting sentences, and concluding sentences when they are learning to writing paragraphs. Encourage students to refer to these when writing independently.

Continued

Grades 6–12

- Provide sentences frames to support students as they practice complex academic language and articulate their understanding of subject-area content.
- Have students speak and write using sentence frames. For example, provide a frame for students to explain how they reached the answer for an equation. "To find the area of the triangle, I used the formula ______. I multiplied one-half times ______ to find the answer ______."
- Project frames are also beneficial. For example, when requiring students to use presentation software, provide a template they can complete with the content they develop.

More for You

Sentence frames are useful for restorative conversations as well. When students are anxious or in a situation that may cause heightened emotions, producing language is even more difficult. Help students by providing sentence starters and phrases they can use during these situations.

Keep in Mind

Students' receptive language skills develop more quickly, while language production takes longer to learn. Producing language can feel riskier, and students' internal editors make them nervous to speak and write due to fear they might make errors. When students are first learning a new language, they go through a silent period during which they are observing and getting used to hearing and understanding the new language. It is critical to be patient and allow students time as they gain confidence.

Organize It

Support the development of students' productive language, both oral and written, with graphic organizers. Use graphic organizers for learning and practicing language and for preparing to write and to speak. Graphic organizers can also be used to guide listening. Providing students with graphic organizers helps them chunk written language and shape and practice oral language.

Make It Real

Grades PK–1

At this stage, graphic organizers should be created together as a class.

- Develop a graphic on chart paper or on the board to guide student learning.
- Model thinking processes when using an organizer. Help students connect their learning from one step to the next.
- Refer back to the graphic organizer to practice and review language and content.
- One graphic organizer to use at this level is a simple table for new vocabulary, with three columns—one for the word, one for a sentence using the word, and one for a drawing of the word. Display it in the classroom and add new words as they are introduced.

Grades 2–5

Students are ready to begin creating and using graphic organizers with support.

- As you model using a graphic organizer to support thinking or as a reference for speaking and listening, have students create their own.
- Explicitly teach the purpose of each graphic organizer. This is especially important for organizers that are more abstract such as those used for brainstorming. Students need instruction on how to take the information in a graphic organizer and develop it into complete ideas and sentences.
- Support students in keeping their graphic organizers stored in notebooks and remembering to use them for reference or review.

Continued

Grades 6–12

Students at this stage can learn a variety of graphic organizers, their names, and their purposes, and begin to access and use them independently.

- Support students in understanding which graphic organizers are best to use depending on the assignment. For example, a mind map is used for brainstorming prior to writing, while a T-chart can be used for a side-by-side comparison.
- Use paper and digital organizers. Paper organizers are good for immediate reference during speaking and listening activities. Digital organizers are good for writing, as information can be more easily transferred between documents.
- Always model how to create and use graphic organizers before expecting students to use them independently.

More for You

Graphic organizers do not have to be pre-created. Having students make their own graphic organizers is an efficient way to save time making copies, and it helps students learn how to create and maintain their own organizers. Model creation of the graphic organizer and have students create their own as they follow along during the lesson.

Keep in Mind

Using a graphic organizer is not always intuitive. Students need explicit instructions on why they are using a graphic organizer, how to use the organizer, and how to transfer the knowledge and organization they gained from creating the organizer onto the next step of speaking or writing.

Content Is Language

Every lesson is a language lesson. As part of learning content, multilingual learners must learn the language for the content. This is especially true in subject areas with complex academic language, such as science and math. It is important to create language goals within content instruction (Fisher and Frey 2010). Identify and plan for the academic vocabulary students are expected to use and understand, as well as the language structures, and teach them explicitly. Create separate learning targets for the language structures and functions. *Language structures* refers to the technical aspects of language, such as vocabulary and sentence structures. *Language functions* refers to how and why language is used. Model language structures and functions and provide opportunities for students to practice together. Repetition is key to students using language correctly and appropriately for the content.

Make It Real

Grades PK–1

Much of what children are learning at these levels is based on factual description and making comparisons across subject areas.

- Teach the academic language related to describing and comparing things, whether they are numbers, events, people, or other topics.
- Teach students the sentence structures used to describe and compare for each content area.
- Students need to know language to understand instructions. For example, for making comparisons, pre-teach vocabulary such as *same*, *different*, and *describe*.

Grades 2–5

These students are engaged in increased critical thinking and abstract thought. They are moving beyond describing, to making predictions, summarizing, and developing their own ideas.

- Teach the language students need to navigate instructions, such as making a prediction, or writing their own narrative. Ensure students know this language prior to giving instructions.
- Pre-teach any academic vocabulary students need to understand a lesson, such as the terms for the task, like *summarize* and *predict*.
- The meaning of terms varies depending on the content. For example, in science we make predictions about what will happen in an experiment, and we use specific sentence structures to state those predictions. We also make predictions in stories and use specific language for those predictions. It is critical to teach these differences to students.

Continued

Grades 6–12

Analysis and synthesis of information is central to learning in secondary grades. Content becomes increasingly complex in language and structure.

- Pre-teaching academic vocabulary is critical. Complex vocabulary should be taught in context and reviewed each time students encounter the words in a new or different context.
- Students need to be explicitly taught the language structures they are expected to use for each content area. For example, students must express math equations using specific sentence structures. Help students articulate their understanding by providing models that incorporate the target academic vocabulary and sentence structures.
- When content requires multiple language structures and functions, break them into parts and teach each element independently.

More for You

English language proficiency (ELP) standards such as the WIDA standards (2020) provide a framework through which to identify language forms and functions. Use ELP standards alongside grade-level content standards to pull out the language within the content.

Keep in Mind

Language learning is most effective in context. Though pre-teaching the language students will encounter during a lesson is important, it is also critical to point out the language within the context of the content as you teach. Pre-teaching and then reteaching during the content lesson will help students learn the language more efficiently.

Make Grammar Real

When we learn our first language as children, we learn grammar passively through daily use and in context. Grammar is not meant to be learned as an isolated subject. When taught in context, grammar becomes meaningful and real. While it is important to teach the rules of language, it is equally important to use real-world language as the vehicle for lessons. Multilingual learners use the grammar that is accepted as correct by their peers and community, in addition to academic grammar. This is where "real-world language" becomes an important tool to ensure students can make those connections.

Make It Real

Grades PK–1

Intentionally embed grammar in lessons.

- Model correct grammar. When students use language incorrectly, instead of saying they are incorrect, simply repeat what they say using correct grammar.
- Have students label visuals with simple grammar elements, for example, prepositions such as *in*, *on*, and *over*.
- Create games, for example, use total physical response to act out prepositions (e.g., "stand in front of your chair").
- Sing grammar songs and add movement for different grammar elements.

Grades 2–5

Students must be able to identify grammar within the texts they are reading and writing.

- Continue to gently model correct grammar when students make errors while speaking.
- Mistakes are a good vehicle for teaching grammar in context. Students can identify grammar errors and fix them in writing and dialogue.
- Have students identify grammar elements through a scavenger hunt or in a song. Use real-world materials to teach grammar.
- Have students practice describing visuals and images using adjectives.

Grades 6–12

Students need to be more independent in recognizing correct grammar and identifying errors.

- Have students engage in conversation as much as possible, especially with their English-speaking classmates, who provide models for correct grammar.
- Teach grammar through editing. Have students look for specific grammar elements in their writing.
- Use content to teach grammar. For example, have students identify grammar elements in story dialogue.
- Discuss the function of grammar in texts or in dialogue.

More for You

Check out the Grammar Songs playlist at the Silly School Education channel on YouTube. The "Question Mark Song" is a favorite!

Keep in Mind

Students will be at different levels of language acquisition regardless of their age or grade level. Since the expectations in the secondary grades are high regardless of a student's language proficiency level, it is essential to help students be as independent as possible and intentionally help them assess their own grammar, especially in their writing.

Bring Life to Language

Students are more interested and better able to learn when they can see the connection between what they are learning and the real world around them. Additionally, for multilingual learners, connecting language to real-world experiences or objects aids in comprehension and language recall. Use realia to help students make these connections. Materials such as maps, menus, and news articles bring learning to life. Primary sources such as diaries, letters, and photos can be used to provide context and history.

Make It Real

Grades PK–1

Bringing life to language should be fun and provoke students' imaginations. Much of what students learn in these early years is concrete, so using realia in lessons makes sense.

- When possible, bring in actual items that correspond to the language being learned. For example, if you are teaching about fruit, bring fruit and related kitchen items.
- Have students interact with the real-world items as they practice the target language.
- Incorporate dramatic play. After practicing as a class, have students act out scenes using the realia and the target language.

Grades 2–5

Immersing students in real-world experiences is highly impactful.

- Field trips provide an excellent opportunity to bring life to language. Field trips can be nearby, even to other parts of the school. Make sure students understand the purpose and have language-related goals to accomplish.
- Role-play using real-world artifacts as props. Use the props for language recall and as language cues. Keep in mind that students are becoming more self-aware, which can cause anxiety. Students do not have to role-play in front of the whole class. Small groups work just as well.

Grades 6–12

Use realia to provide context, as props to support conversation, or as resources for writing or debate. Use real-world items to illustrate mathematical or scientific concepts.

- Provide items students can reference while practicing language. For example, use maps when learning to give and receive directions.
- Primary sources are beneficial when discussing history, reading nonfiction texts, and writing. Oral histories, photographs, newspaper articles, and journal entries are particularly useful as they are often shorter or offer a visual component.

More for You

When it is not possible to bring in real-life items to support students' learning, technology and the internet offer access to the world and real-life examples through images, stories, and videos.

Keep in Mind

Realia should not simply be a prop or a visual. It should be something students can interact with and use as they are learning.

Teach It in Pictures

Visuals help students understand and remember language. When students can connect language to what they see and experience, they are more likely to learn. Use visuals as much as possible to support instruction. Visuals move beyond images to physical models and body movement.

Make It Real

Grades PK–1

Visuals are common when teaching these levels; look for opportunities to use them even more often.

- Make sure visuals are concrete. Abstract connections are difficult for young children to make.
- When teaching vocabulary, whenever possible, use an image to clarify the meaning of the word(s).
- Provide visuals when giving instructions. Visuals can be more than pictures and can include physically modeling expectations.
- Use models and manipulatives during math and science instruction.

Grades 2–5

Include students in creating visuals, with support from you.

- Have students create visuals to support their own language learning. Use these visuals in the classroom environment, just as you would display teacher- or professionally made visuals.
- Provide students with space on assignments to create visual representations of their learning.
- Use chart paper to illustrate language. Display the charts in the classroom throughout a lesson or unit.
- Use models and manipulatives to support students' learning.

Grades 6–12

Provide strategies students can use to create their own visuals to support their learning.

- Visual dictionaries are a good resource for students. Teach students to create their own dictionaries of words and phrases accompanied by visuals that are personally meaningful to them.
- Use models and manipulatives when possible for content with complex academic language.
- Visually model expectations when giving instructions and teaching new content.
- Incorporate visual elements into projects and assignments.

Keep in Mind

Visuals to support multilingual learners include pictures, time lines, charts and graphs, examples of opposites, cloze sentences, and realia (FluentU 2023). Visuals do not have universal meaning. Ensure that any visuals you use represent the languages of students you are teaching. For example, stop signs, while used in most countries, are not the same in every nation. Therefore, if you have students who come from nations in which the red octagonal sign is not the symbol for stop, it would not be a good visual for the word *stop*.

Get Moving

Movement enhances brain functioning and helps multilingual learners make language connections. Total physical response (TPR) is the use of movement in conjunction with learning to solidify comprehension. TPR not only helps students learn language, it is engaging and improves their recall. It supports language acquisition as students connect physical movement and language by acting out language or responding to it (Asher 2009). Movement does not have to involve the whole body. Ensure the movement you incorporate into your lessons is manageable for every student.

Make It Real

Grades PK–1

- Help students learn verbs through TPR. Students do the action for the verb or phrase you call out.
- Teach students songs that include movement to reinforce and practice target language.
- Play games that include movement. Draw stick pictures of target vocabulary on each section of a volleyball. Have students stand in a circle and toss the ball to one another. When they catch the ball, they look at the picture facing them and make a sentence using the word for the picture.

Grades 2–5

- TPR and songs are also effective at these grade levels. Have students create some of the movements themselves.
- Students at these levels enjoy friendly competition. Incorporate opportunities for movement combined with competition, such as coming to the board to write answers.
- Charades allows students to use their bodies to represent language and provides opportunities to orally produce language as classmates guess what their peers' movements represent.

Grades 6–12

- These students may resist movement, but persevere, as they thoroughly enjoy the opportunity to move rather than sit at desks. When practicing conversation with classmates, have students stand.
- Ensure that the actions make sense in context to lower the social risks of participating. Movement in response to content questions is effective. For example, assign each student a phase of migration. Then state facts students learned about the different phases. When a fact falls within the phase a student was assigned, they stand.

More for You

I have had success using the American Sign language (ASL) alphabet when teaching letters and spelling and using signs for different vocabulary words. This strategy helped my students remember letters and words. Additionally, using basic ASL was especially helpful to my neurodiverse multilingual learners and is inclusive of students who are hard of hearing or deaf.

Make It a Game

Creating an immersive game in your classroom is motivating for students and helps them track their learning. Additionally, simply using games to teach language engages students and helps them enjoy learning. Games make learning fun and increase student confidence. You can set up a game with a storyline, goals, and badges as a way for students to track their progress. Establish goals that relate to content-area objectives and language objectives, and have students collect badges as they meet the goals. Teacher-created (and sometimes student-created) board or card games can also be used to support students' learning and mastery of language.

Make It Real

Grades PK–1

Young students love to use their imaginations. Games provide an opportunity to tap into those imaginations and help students learn in context.

- Create an immersive experience for students with specific language and content goals in mind. For example, create a camping scene in your classroom with a focus on learning nouns, verbs, and the language used for being in the outdoors. Students can go on a "trip" through the classroom, practicing language along the way.
- As students journey through the experience, they earn stickers or stamps for demonstrating their learning, such as using the target sentence or vocabulary correctly.
- Basic games increase engagement too. For example, place students in two teams. One at a time, students race to the board to draw a picture of an alphabet letter or a vocabulary word the teacher says. The winner collects points for their team.

Grades 2–5

Students at these levels are engaged when tangible rewards are attached to learning goals.

- Create a classroom game during which students collect badges and move to new levels and challenges based on content and language mastery. Students must overcome challenges to collect points toward a goal. One example is an escape room. Teams of students must work together to solve problems and get clues to "unlock" the classroom and escape.
- Have students collect and track the badges or points they earn. This makes learning fun and helps students track their progress. Students can earn badges for achieving academic goals and collect the badges to earn a reward.
- Repurpose familiar games such as charades or board games to practice target language and content.

Continued

Grades 6–12

Students at these levels are expected to be more independent in their learning, as well as to work in teams. Incorporating technology is common.

- Use technology to allow students to collect digital badges for their learning.
- Have students create their own games using target content and language (words and structures) and then teach and play the games with their classmates. This is a good culminating project through which students can demonstrate their learning.

More for You

Learn more ways to use games in the classroom from the experts. Start with the TedxTalk "The Fastest Growing Demographic for Video Games May Surprise You!" by gamification expert Tammie Schrader (available on YouTube). For more ideas, see Michele Haiken's "5 Ways to Gamify Your Classroom" at iste.org/blog/5-ways-to-gamify-your-classroom.

Keep in Mind

Although creating a game in your classroom takes time, once it is developed, it will be easier to set up for future classes. Plus, the student engagement generated by using games ultimately saves time because students will enjoy learning and will learn more efficiently.

Learning through Projects

Projects are an excellent way to teach content and language in tandem. Projects tap into multilingual learners' interests, are hands-on, and provide opportunities for them to interact with their English-speaking peers and practice the target language (Colorín Colorado, n.d.). Projects are most impactful when expectations are clearly established yet students are given a level of choice within the project to guide their own learning. When using projects with MLs, instruction must be explicit, with specific guidance on expectations and how to collaborate; directions need to be visual; and all related materials should be accessible for students' language proficiency levels (Wolpert-Gawron 2018). It is critical to ensure that the project itself is accessible to MLs, with options for participation that are meaningful and appropriate for their language abilities.

Make It Real

Grades PK–1

Projects at this level are teacher-guided, with steps toward a clearly defined outcome.

- Students are learning inquiry, problem-solving, and factual description. Combine these elements into an overall project through which students can use language in connection with content to demonstrate learning.
- Use projects as end-of-unit assessments. Combine group projects with performances to give students opportunities to demonstrate their understanding through multiple modalities.
- Projects at this level are best completed as a whole class, with students completing some components as a group and small pieces independently.
- An example is having students work together to create a book of what they learn throughout a unit of instruction. During the unit, have students create small pieces of the final product. At the close of the unit, they combine the pieces to have a complete record of their learning. MLs can be responsible for creating the pieces of the project directly related to content language.

Grades 2–5

At these levels, students need clear instructions with guided choices.

- Give students a menu of options for the topic and the type of project they will create.
- Define the content and skills students need to demonstrate.
- For each step, provide students with clear expectations connected to the content and skills outcomes. Students need to know exactly what is expected of them throughout the project.
- Set mile markers for students to help them track their progress.
- An example is creating a flag that represents the class. Leading up to the group effort, students can learn about flags from around the world. MLs can research and present the significance of the flag from the country where they were born. If an ML was born in the United States, they can present the flag from their family's country of origin.

Continued

Grades 6–12

Students at this level need clear, easy-to-follow rubrics and the opportunity to choose their own topics to meet the expectations outlined in the rubrics.

- Projects are effective capstones for end-of-term demonstrations of learning. For each unit of instruction, students complete a piece that will be one part of the final project.
- Older students need more autonomy, so offering choice throughout a project is essential. Students can choose the topic and the medium for completing the project (e.g., slide deck, art project, written report, and so on).
- An example is publishing a class literary magazine. Students contribute written pieces or art created during the semester. Students work together to move through the publishing process, from selecting work, to layout and design, to a final publication that they create and disseminate.

More for You

Projects lend themselves to cross-curricular connections, especially at the elementary level when students have a single teacher for all subjects. Students connect learning across subjects in a time-efficient way, as students can practice and demonstrate their learning through a single culminating project.

Keep in Mind

Complex projects should be divided into parts. Break down the project's components, providing instructions for each part as students progress through the project. Revisit the Step by Step strategy (page 30) for more information.

Expand Access to Technology

Technology can enhance language instruction and provide opportunities for students to practice their learning and gain deeper understanding. Technology can also help facilitate connections between teachers and students, students and students, and students across the globe. Support multilingual learners in using technology such as learning management systems, collaboration software, school gradebooks, and email and messaging with their teachers.

Make It Real

Grades PK–1

Young students may be familiar with screens but have limited experience using them to learn.

- Start students using computer-based learning platforms to practice basic language skills.
- Touchscreen-type devices such as iPads are especially good, as young students often struggle with manipulating keyboards, mice, and trackpads.
- Use a smartboard with programs such as Zoom to connect with other classrooms. Have students play interactive digital games to practice language.

Grades 2–5

Students begin to learn using district-adopted learning platforms. They need direct instruction on using these platforms.

- Ensure students understand the purpose of the learning platform and know how the technology can support their progress.
- Facilitate teacher-student connections using technology. Interact with students using district platforms such as Class Notebook in Teams or Google Classroom.
- Teach digital literacy explicitly. Teach students how to use the available technology and how to find their own.
- Teach students about digital citizenship and how to interact positively with others via technology.
- Reading A-Z, Lexia®, and typing.com are a few online programs to support students in their language and content learning.

Continued

Grades 6–12

Many schools have a one-to-one program, allowing students to carry devices between home and school. Students need guidance in using devices and resources meaningfully.

- Teach students how to navigate information on the internet and how to determine credible sources and identify confirmation bias.
- Teach students how to use technology to build positive connections, how to interact civilly online, and how to identify cyberbullying.
- Engage students in using technology for class projects and assignments.
- Help students use technology to track their own progress.

More for You

Despite technology's prevalence in classrooms, planning for and effectively using it can feel overwhelming. Collaborate with other teachers in your grade level or content area to develop plans to use technology in your classrooms. Develop networks both within your own school and community and outside of your community via social networks or other online-based educator communities. Collaboration with other teachers is also useful in developing cross-curricular and cross-classroom connections.

Keep in Mind

Access is equity. Before asking students to complete assignments or projects, or to practice language via technology at home, ensure every student has access to devices, programs, and internet service.

Listen and Retell

Retelling after listening helps students with listening and speaking proficiency. Retelling also aids working memory, vocabulary acquisition, and comprehension (Kelley, n.d.). In pairs, groups, or individually, when students listen to a passage, conversation, lecture, or story, have them retell what they heard in their own words.

Make It Real

Grades PK–1

Listening and retelling is a natural fit for the PK–1 classroom. Make retelling a common practice when students are listening to understand.

- Young students need support when retelling. Offer questions students can answer that will demonstrate they understood what they heard.
- Storytime is a good opportunity to practice retelling. Listening for understanding is difficult for MLs. When reading aloud, pause briefly throughout the story to chunk the information and allow MLs to process. Ask a question about what students heard and have them share their responses with partners.
- Retelling is a good strategy for reviewing directions. After giving oral instructions, have students retell the expectations. This chunks the instructions into pieces, helping ensure access for MLs.

Grades 2–5

Retelling is an effective strategy for every subject. Students can process their new learning through retelling.

- In math, ask students to retell to partners how to complete a math equation. Students can also use retelling to articulate their understanding of word problems.
- Ask students to retell scientific processes. For example, if students are learning about plants, they can retell the process through which seeds grow into plants.
- In social studies, ask students to retell the events in a timeline or a historical story.
- Use retelling in conversation or storytelling. Retelling to a partner supports MLs with more limited English language proficiency by lessening the pressure. Have one student tell another student a personal narrative and have the listener retell what they remember from their partner's story. Provide a guide that lists what should be included in the story to support the process and help students listen carefully.

Grades 6–12

As classroom content becomes more complex with high academic expectations for MLs at all proficiency levels, retelling is a necessity for checking comprehension.

- Build in opportunities for retelling during direct instruction. Have students share their notes with classmates periodically throughout the instruction.
- Incorporate retelling when reading is assigned as homework. Begin the next class day in groups and have students share what they learned from their reading the night before. Assign shorter passages to MLs with limited English language proficiency, or allow them to retell in their first language. Provide specific questions about the reading that they can use to support retelling.
- Retelling can be a form of formative assessment. During independent work time, check in with students and have them retell what they learned during the lesson.

More for You

The 3-2-1 strategy is an effective way to help students understand and talk about a text (Shapiro 2022). Students share three key points; two connections to themselves, the world, or other texts; and one question they have.

Keep in Mind

Using this strategy should be connected to what is already planned for the class. The strategy is intended to be an extension that does not require significant additional planning. Anytime students are expected to listen for understanding during direct instruction, during a read-aloud, during a class discussion, or when viewing a video or listening to a recording, take time to pause and have students retell what they heard.

Talk It Out

To learn content, multilingual learners need everyday practice with listening and speaking. Provide oral language practice during every lesson, incorporating opportunities for students to practice the academic language connected to their content learning. Practice can include whole-class question and answer with volunteers, using sentence frames and graphic organizers to articulate learning, discussion in groups or pairs, and reading student writing aloud.

Make It Real

Grades PK–1

Students in the early grades need highly structured opportunities to practice oral language.

- Every lesson should include oral language practice. Some students are not yet ready to produce full sentences on their own. Whole-class practice using choral response is an effective strategy.
- Be specific about the expectations when students are practicing oral language. Have students practice language by repeating after you. Only after this repetition should students use the language independently.
- Keep oral language practice simple, incorporating only the academic language relevant to the content of instruction.

Grades 2–5

Students are expected to present their learning more often as they progress through grade levels. As students learn new academic language and skills, they need regular practice speaking about their learning.

- "Turn and talk" is a quick way for students to practice language they just learned. During lessons, have students turn and talk with partners to discuss what was just learned.
- Have students write sentences incorporating the target content language and sharing what they learned. The sentences can be shared with partners or this can be a more formal assignment. It can also be used for content review.
- Whenever possible, have students present their written work or projects to the class. For oral presentations, provide specific guidelines for how and what to share with the class.

Grades 6–12

Learning in the upper grades is often writing-focused. Intentionally incorporating oral language practice into lessons supports MLs.

- Use whole-class or group discussions to provide content-related oral language practice. Prepare students for participation in discussions by teaching students how to use notes and other materials as references.
- Explicitly teach students how to engage in whole-class discussions. Assign specific roles or specific content elements to students to help them plan for participation.
- Turn and talks are also effective in these grades. Any opportunity for students to discuss their learning with classmates is beneficial.

More for You

In second grade and higher, when students can write proficiently enough, structure math practice to include writing answers using full sentences and academic language. Have students read these sentences aloud to partners. This gives students practice using mathematical language orally, and it is an opportunity for them to check their answers with classmates. Do the same for other subjects.

Keep in Mind

To master academic language, students must engage daily with the target language through the four main language domains. They need to hear the language, use the language orally and in writing, and read the language. However, be patient with students still in the silent period who resist speaking. Allow them to participate in a different way, such as drawing a response or responding physically to demonstrate understanding. Trust that they are gaining receptive language skills and will try speaking when they are ready.

Oral Language Prompts

Producing language orally takes confidence. Teaching correct phrasing, especially in academic contexts, supports multilingual learners as they produce language. Provide sentence frames such as questions and sentence starters to help students have the confidence to engage in conversations using class content and target language.

Make It Real

Grades PK–1

- Model the oral language students should use. Have students repeat phrases after you several times and practice in pairs.
- Use realia as an oral language prompt. Use a simple question frame students can remember, such as "What is this?" Then have students use a real item, such as a pencil, to prompt the response. The student holds up the pencil and says, "This is a pencil."
- Sit in a circle and have realia available from a unit of instruction, such as items in a school. Give each student an item or have students pass the same item around the circle. One student holds up the item, says what it is, and shows or says how it is used. For example, a student holds up a pencil and says, "This is a pencil." The student then pretends to write with it and says, "I write with a pencil."
- Distribute pictures of items related to a topic. Describe one of them. The student with the matching picture holds it up. When students are more comfortable with the content, have them respond with a sentence as they hold up the picture.

Grades 2–5

- When introducing a topic, provide questions for students to ask one another, such as, "What did you learn about this topic last year?" Provide sentence starters to help students answer, such as, "Last year I learned __________."
- Provide prompts asking for and offering support to peers. For example, "How do you spell…?" and "Can I help you spell that word?" Practice these with students and work to create a culture in which students are comfortable asking for and giving help.
- When asking students to discuss academic content in groups, provide language prompts, especially sentence starters that help students begin conversing about a topic. For example, if students are learning about the planets, provide sentence starters that help students remember details, such as, "The fourth planet from the sun is _____." "Two characteristics of the sun are _____ and _____."

Continued

Grades 6–12

- For any whole-class or small-group discussions, provide students with content-specific oral language prompts. These can be simple sentence starters based on the content to be discussed.
- Have MLs in the earlier stages of language proficiency ask rather than answer the questions during discussions. Provide pre-written questions for these students. Using pre-planned questions is not as heavy of a lift. Being the questioner still stretches a student's abilities, though, as they must choose appropriate questions to ask based on the flow of the discussion.
- Oral language prompts are also beneficial for conversation in pairs. When students discuss what they learned from an activity, an assignment, or a reading, oral language prompts help them articulate their understanding, which supports comprehension. Create prompts to help students focus on and discuss the important information they learned.

More for You

Oral language prompts can be used during get-to-know-you activities. Provide question prompts and sentence starters for students to use to learn more about one another. Oral language prompts are also beneficial during restorative conversations.

Keep in Mind

There is social risk when MLs participate in academic conversations when they are not yet comfortable speaking English. They may feel nervous that they will make a mistake or embarrassed when they do make a mistake. Oral language prompts help students feel less insecure and more willing to participate.

Authentic Language

Multilingual learners benefit from hearing multiple examples of natural language in context. Authentic language refers to language used in everyday contexts and by different speakers. Students need to hear a variety of models. This means exposing students to different accents and language used in contexts other than the classroom. Use materials that provide authentic language examples such as podcasts and short videos. Ensure that the media is related to content students are learning. These examples will help students understand how the subject is discussed or referenced in conversations in the real world and will provide a model they can emulate.

Make It Real

Grades PK–1

Many videos and recordings are available for young learners.

- First assess media for authentic language use and ease of comprehension.
- Check to confirm the media does not have excessive background noise and the speaker or performer communicates at an appropriate speed.
- After students have listened to the media, check for understanding.

Grades 2–5

Many videos and other media are available for the middle elementary grades.

- Curriculum, especially curriculum for MLs, often comes with media that includes authentic language examples. If the examples are beneficial to students, utilize them.
- Invite other teachers or support staff to come in and model language with you. MLs benefit from hearing different accents and different ways of speaking.

Grades 6–12

Content-specific videos and podcasts will deepen understanding and extend learning.

- Prepare students for listening by previewing what they will hear. Create a listening guide with questions that cue students to what they should be listening for. This guide can then be used for review.
- Incorporate choice by providing a list of vetted media from which students can select.

More for You

Classmates who are native speakers of English are a good resource for authentic language practice and exposure. Create opportunities for MLs to listen to presentations by and converse with their English-speaking peers.

Keep in Mind

Students need to know the purpose for listening and what to listen for. If the content is complex, pre-teach vocabulary and provide a listening guide. Listening to authentic language is difficult because natural speech is fast, and words often run together. When students understand the context and have an idea of what they will hear, they are better able to understand it.

Real Talk Prep

Speaking in a new language can cause nervousness and anxiety. Preparing students to engage in conversation helps ease these feelings. Preparation includes instruction on active listening, how to ask and answer questions, and asking follow-up questions, as well as addressing nonverbal communication. Modeling and practicing conversations is also helpful.

Make It Real

Grades PK–1

At these levels, focus on facial expressions and nonverbal responses.

- Help students connect language to nonverbal cues. Practice making facial expressions that match feeling words. Have students play emotions charades. A student chooses a word and portrays that emotion with their face and body language. Other students guess the emotion.
- Display pictures of people and have students describe what the people's facial expressions and other cues tell them about what the people are feeling.
- Match tone and facial expression to emotion. Model for students how people adjust the tone they use depending on what they are saying. Have students practice matching their tone to emotions.

Grades 2–5

In addition to reading nonverbal cues, students also need to begin to understand two-way communication and asking and answering questions.

- Have students practice active listening by building on one another's responses. Give students a topic to discuss. One student listens and asks questions, and the other student answers. The listener asks questions based on what their partner says.
- Explain the importance of asking follow-up questions to learn more and to better understand what people are telling them. Model how to ask follow-up questions.
- Have students practice asking follow-up questions. Provide initial question prompts related to the lesson content to help students start their conversations.

Grades 6–12

Students in secondary grades need support in all the areas younger students require, but with a particular focus on academic conversations.

- Explicitly teach students how to develop questions based on what they seek to know about a topic. At the close of a lesson, have students write one or two clarifying questions. Start the next lesson by having students ask their questions. Use this as a review of the previous learning.
- Explicitly teach students how to ask follow-up questions to extend their understanding during discussions. Require students to ask at least one follow-up question for every initial question they ask. Teach students to ask clarifying questions when they do not understand the whole response. For example, in English class, when discussing a novel they might ask, "Who was the main character?" After the answer, they would then ask, "How do you know _____ is the main character?" Follow-up questions are intended to expand understanding and clarify information.

More for You

When teaching students about nonverbal communication, you have an opportunity to bring culture into the classroom. Explore the differences in nonverbal communication between cultures. Allow students to share examples of nonverbal communication from their heritage cultures. When students in higher grades are learning persuasion, argumentation can result in heated and emotional exchanges. Teach students appropriate demeanor during an argument and how to identify the nonverbal cues that suggest someone is becoming sad, frustrated, or angry.

Keep in Mind

While similar to oral language prompts, this type of preparation moves beyond support during whole-class or small-group discussions to supporting students in recognizing, understanding, and using culturally appropriate nonverbal communication depending on the context, and in engaging in active two-way communication.

Write What I Say

Dictation is a strategy that helps multilingual learners listen for understanding and learn grammatical structures. Dictation can be done as a whole class, with a partner, or independently. Determine the goal of the dictation and what you are looking for, whether it is punctuation, spelling, or writing complete sentences. Model the process for the class. Dictate a sentence, passage, or directions to students and have them write what you say.

Make It Real

Grades PK–1

- Dictating letters by sound helps students connect the image of the letter and the sound the letter makes.
- Move on to single-word dictation. Much like a spelling test, this can be used to assess how accurately students are hearing letter sounds. Words that can be spelled phonetically are best.
- Dictating can also be used to practice very short sentences when students are ready.

Grades 2–5

- In addition to spelling dictation, have students write complete sentences that you dictate. Ensure the dictation is relevant to the class content.
- When students are ready, have them begin to expand on the dictation by adding another detail or sentence or filling in missing information.
- Use dictation for simple instructions. Have students write each step as you say it. This is good practice for learning how to receive directions.

Grades 6–12

- Use dictation for conversation practice to provide a model for language, example phrasing, and word choice.
- Use dictation at the beginning of writing assignments to get students started. Dictate the first one or two sentences, then have students continue the writing on their own.
- Have students dictate to partners. They take turns stating information that the receiver needs to write down. For example, giving directions to a place or providing an address.

More for You

Dictation can be used for formative assessment. Review students' responses to determine their individual strengths and to identify areas for additional practice. Another assessment option is to dictate questions for older students to write and then answer in their own words.

Keep in Mind

Having students dictate to one another should only be used when students have good English pronunciation skills. Accurate pronunciation is critical, therefore, only have students dictate to one another when they are at higher language proficiency levels.

Efficient Listening

When learning a new language, it can be difficult to follow oral communication because native speakers of the language often speak quickly and string words together. Support multilingual learners in listening efficiently to understand the gist of a conversation. Much like deciphering word problems or complex texts by identifying the most important information and disregarding the rest, students need to learn to listen with intention, picking out the important phrases and words.

Make It Real

Grades PK–1

At these levels, use simple checks for understanding during read-alouds and periodically throughout instruction.

- When reading aloud to students, after each event in the story, pause and ask questions about what happened. Guide students via questioning to identify the important information in the story.
- Use the same strategy during instruction. Divide instruction into parts and pause after each part to check for understanding through guided questioning.

Grades 2–5

At these grade levels, use simple checks for understanding, as well as providing explicit instruction on identifying what is essential information and what is not.

- During read-alouds, guide students in listening for important information. Use the Think Out Loud strategy (page 33) to demonstrate how to listen efficiently.
- During direct instruction, remind students of the main topic and vocabulary. Give them context for what they are about to hear. Pause periodically to review and help students identify the essential elements of what they heard.
- Have students engage in teacher-created dialogues or conversations provided in the curriculum. Model how to listen for key words and phrases to find clues to the meaning. Then have students watch or listen to a conversation and work together in pairs or groups to determine the main points. After students have practiced, have them decipher conversations independently.

Grades 6–12

In secondary grades, students need additional support to listen efficiently during direct instruction and class discussions. Classes at the secondary level frequently employ these modes of teaching.

- Prior to instruction or a discussion, review what students have learned and highlight key terms and phrases they should listen for during the lesson. One idea is to provide BINGO cards with these key terms or phrases and have students mark the terms when they hear them to get a BINGO.
- Guide class discussions to ensure students stay on topic. When students do go astray, quickly guide them back to the topic at hand. Before allowing a discussion to continue, remind students of what has already been said to recontextualize the discussion.
- Pause regularly to check for understanding. Retelling is a good way to practice identifying key points during a lesson.

More for You

Utilize prerecorded conversations for listening practice. English language acquisition curriculum often provides pre-recorded conversations, or you can create them. You can also find them online—YouTube has a variety of conversations for use with multilingual learners. In addition, have students listen to audiobooks to support their reading skills and to practice efficient listening.

Keep in Mind

Explicitly teach vernacular or common phrases people use when they are trying to think of what they might say next, such as, “you know what I mean,” or “like.” Help students identify these types of phrases, so they can listen “around” them to find the key points in a conversation or discussion.

Take a Position

Argumentation is an engaging way to teach and practice language. Debate requires quick responses and ignites passion in the participants as they defend their positions. Constructing structured arguments helps multilingual learners plan language in advance, enabling them to respond more readily to their opponents' arguments. Consider the language proficiency levels of MLs to determine the complexity of argumentation to engage in and the topics to address. For MLs with limited English language proficiency, use topics with less technical language. To engage students, combine the language structures for academic argumentation with topics that are more social in nature, but still content related.

Make It Real

Grades PK–1

Students are learning to share their opinions in a socially productive way. Keep argumentation simple at this stage.

- Teach students the language for sharing their opinions and providing at least one reason for their opinions. Teach language structures such as "I like…" or "My favorite…"
- Teach students how to agree or disagree with an opinion and provide at least one reason. Teach language structures such as "I also like…" or "I do not like… I like…"
- Students can practice sharing their opinions with one another about content topics, such as their favorite story.
- At this stage students should not be working to persuade. They should be working only to share their opinions and listen respectfully to the opinions of others.

Grades 2–5

Students at these levels are beginning to organize information, learn facts, and add supporting details.

- Teach students the language for supporting a statement of fact. For example, if students are learning about migration, teach them how to make a statement of fact, such as, "Changes in the climate led to early migration on the continent of Africa." They then provide details to support their claim.
- Build on statements of fact by having students assert opinions, followed by two or three statements of fact, with one or two supporting details for each fact.
- Have students present their arguments in a compare-and-contrast format with individuals or groups offering one opinion and then the next group offering a different opinion.

Continued

Grades 6–12

Structured debate provides students in secondary grades with the opportunity to plan what they will say using high-level academic language and then say exactly what they planned. This preparation helps students have more confidence when they must respond to their opponent's arguments with less planning.

- Have teams of students (usually pairs) plan structured debate arguments, with half taking one side and half taking the other side. Explain the structure of the debate and the structure of the arguments.
- Provide students time for research and writing to prepare for the debate.
- Model debate for students using videos.

More for You

Use Four Corners to have students practice using their learning to support their opinions. Post the following labels in the four corners of the room: strongly agree, agree, disagree, strongly disagree. Make a statement, and then have students move to the corner of the room that corresponds to their stance. Students in each corner discuss reasons to support their opinion. The whole class then discusses the statement, and each group defends its opinion.

Keep in Mind

Argumentation based on complex topics with highly technical language is best suited for multilingual learners who are at a higher English language proficiency level. Students need to have a firm foundation in English before you should expect them to engage in spontaneous debate.

Mirror, Mirror

Speaking English often requires multilingual learners to use their muscles in new ways to make specific lip and tongue movements. It is essential to teach students how to shape words and sounds with their mouths. Demonstrate how the parts of the mouth move to form words and letter sounds. For practice, have students look in mirrors to focus on how their mouths move when making letter and word sounds.

Make It Real

Grades PK–1

- Give each student a handheld mirror. Mirrors should be easy for students to hold and large enough so they can see their whole face.
- Overexaggerate the mouth shapes and movements for letter sounds. Have students look at themselves in the mirrors while trying to mimic your mouth movements to make the sounds on their own.
- After teaching individual letter sounds, help students connect letter sounds to form words.
- Younger students may be easily distracted by the mirrors. Keep lessons short to ensure the focus is on using the mirrors for pronunciation practice.

Grades 2–5

- Each student should be provided with their own mirror if possible. However, shared mirrors can work at this level as students are not yet highly self-conscious.
- Model by exaggerating the mouth movements and forms for each letter and word sound. Have students copy you while using the mirrors to look at themselves.
- Regularly review the letter sounds using mirrors. Each time new sound combinations are introduced or anytime students are learning new words or phrases, use the mirrors to practice.

Grades 6–12

- Mirrors should be just large enough for students to see their mouths, chins, and cheeks. Smaller mirrors can help students focus on forming sounds rather than on what their faces look like, which can make students feel embarrassed.
- Demonstrate the mouth formation for the letter or word. Exaggerate the mouth movements. Have students use the mirrors to observe their own mouths forming the letter or word.
- Once students have mastered basic letter and word sounds, revisit this strategy any time you introduce more complex and difficult-to-pronounce language.

Keep in Mind

Using mirrors for pronunciation is a good strategy for *all* students learning letters and words in the early grades, and also supports students learning more complex, technical vocabulary in the upper grades.

Targeted Reading Materials

Complex texts can be challenging for multilingual learners to navigate. Support students by providing reading materials that build background knowledge and align with their language and reading proficiency levels. These materials do not replace class texts but support learning by ensuring students have access to the content at a language level they can understand. If possible, use Lexile reading levels and language proficiency levels to determine the supplemental materials to provide.

Make It Real

Grades PK–1

For these students in particular, comprehensible input can include materials to support understanding that are not word based.

- Depending on language and reading level, provide written content for students as they are ready. Begin with pictures that match the written content, move from single words to short sentences, then to longer sentences and short paragraphs.
- Provide informational texts at students' reading levels as well as other materials to support comprehension, such as pictures or realia that align with content.

Grades 2–5

Provide materials that are accessible for different language proficiency levels.

- In addition to curriculum texts, provide supplemental materials that are comprehensible at varying reading levels and that teach the content. Allow all students to access these materials regardless of their language proficiency levels.
- For independent reading, while it is good to help students identify books that are accessible to them, it is also important to allow students to choose books they would like to read. Independently choosing books to read for pleasure is critical for nurturing the love of reading.

Grades 6–12

Students are expected to navigate complex and dense texts regardless of language proficiency levels.

- Explicitly teach how to use the resources for an assignment. For example, for document-based questions, provide various materials, such as artwork, tables and graphs, personal narratives, and short paragraphs, along with the original text
- Provide access to materials at varying reading levels and allow all students to choose which materials to use.
- For independent reading, provide a range of levels and genres. For example, picture books written for older students, graphic novels, middle grade and young adult books, and novels.

Keep in Mind

Regardless of language proficiency level, students must have access to the same learning and resources as their peers who are native speakers of English. Accommodate language proficiency by providing supplemental materials, adding instructional supports, and allowing for a variety of modes for demonstrating content proficiency (see Supportive Assessment, pages 89–95 for ideas).

Interview a Text

Help multilingual students become independent readers by explicitly teaching the elements of a text and how to use them to make predictions about it. Before reading, activate students' focus by previewing the text. Look at the title, any images or graphics, and any other text elements. The first several times, do this with the whole class. When it is clear students understand how to interview a text, they can do so in small groups or independently. Provide a "text interview" guide for students to write notes about each element of the text, then make a prediction. Predictions for informational texts should include accessing students' prior knowledge. Tap into students' funds of knowledge by asking them to brainstorm what they already know about the topic that is addressed in the text.

Make It Real

Grades PK–1

Before beginning a new read-aloud, have students practice making predictions.

- Interpreting the images in picture books is an essential skill for students. Help students look at visuals critically. Guide them in seeing all the parts of the pictures to understand the story.
- Ask students specific questions about the pictures. For example, "How does the child in the picture feel?" "How do you know?" "Based the child's feelings, what do you think will happen in this part of the story?"
- You may wish to preview all the images in a book. Ask students, "After looking at the pictures, what do you think will happen in this book?"
- You do not need to have students to make predictions every time you read a story. Reserve some read-alouds for simple enjoyment.

Grades 2–5

Pictures and chapter titles are the main means through which to make predictions in these grades. Pictures include cover art and art at the beginning of chapters (if present).

- Model for students how to make predictions prior to reading a text. After you have modeled several times, make predictions together as a group about the text.
- Provide students with graphic organizers to guide them when making predictions. The organizer can include all the text elements (e.g., book title, cover art, chapter titles, and interior pictures). Provide space for students to write about the different elements and space for them to explain what they think the text is about.
- Ask guiding questions to help students make predictions, such as, "What does the title tell us about the story?"

Continued

Grades 6–12

Making predictions at this stage should include all text elements, including any cover text and features at the back of a book, such as a glossary or appendices.

- Break textbooks into sections and have students look at all the text elements prior to reading the section. They should look at bold words, graphs and charts, and images to make their predictions.
- When reading novels or narrative nonfiction books, teach students how to use the book synopsis on the back cover or on the jacket flap to learn about what they might read. Based on that information, have students predict what they think might happen in the story.

More for You

Making predictions can be used to prepare students for other types of material. Previewing and making predictions about videos they will view, audio they will listen to, or conversations and discussions they will participate in supports students as they learn from different resources.

Keep in Mind

Students need guidance as they learn to make predictions productively. Model making predictions even in the upper grades. Students need several examples before they can effectively make predictions that serve their learning.

Reading Guide

Understanding the purpose for reading helps multilingual learners focus and better discern important information. Explain why a text is relevant to what students are learning and give a general purpose for reading it. To support MLs, provide a reading guide with comprehension questions that help them find the information they need. As students' language proficiency increases, ask questions about both what is directly in the text and what students can infer. Always consider students' language proficiency levels when developing a reading guide, and adjust levels of support for navigating a text as needed.

Make It Real

Grades PK–1

Ask targeted questions periodically during whole-class reading.

- Prior to reading aloud, ask a question that MLs should think about as they listen. After reading, ask students if they heard the answer.
- When MLs are ready for more independent reading, provide a question they must answer. Have them work with partners to determine the answer.
- Include questions that require thinking beyond what is directly in the text and include students' own connections.

Grades 2–5

Teach students what different types of questions are asking.

- Ask questions that help students identify important ideas in the text, check for understanding, and connect what they are learning across texts and to other learning.
- For independent reading, create a guide that focuses on the target information. Include questions that ask students to apply the information to their learning. End with a question that helps students think about what learning may happen next.

Grades 6–12

Analysis and synthesis are key skills for these students.

- Support students in identifying key pieces of information in the text, then guide them in using that information for analysis and synthesis.
- Have students work in groups to complete reading guides. They can work together on the more complicated questions. In this way, students have increased access to complex texts, and they are checking their answers, making the reading guide useful as a study guide or as notes for a project or assignment.

More for You

Write reading guides so that each question builds on the next. Begin with a question that asks MLs to locate information directly in the text, and then gradually increase the difficulty, asking students to think more critically with each subsequent question.

Keep in Mind

Consider allowing students to complete the reading guide in their first language. Using the first language to process information increases the likelihood that students will understand the content and be able to access it later. Using the first language also helps with transfer of skills to the new language.

Read It Together

Multilingual learners are at varied reading levels and have different degrees of comfort with reading, but all students need access to all texts in the classroom—from items on display such as classroom expectations, to directions, to instructional texts. For such texts, support MLs by using a variety of strategies that increase access and decrease anxiety about reading. Read aloud to the class, have students read together as a class via choral reading, or read in groups, with each member or pair reading part of the text aloud. Be sure to create mixed-level groups, with low and high English language proficiency and native speakers of English in a group. Consider the proficiency levels when assigning roles during group reading as well.

Make It Real

Grades PK–1

All students benefit from low-risk reading opportunities such as choral reading.

- Having students recite letters and sounds together is a way to support MLs as they learn these essential elements of reading.
- Learning new words and phrases offers opportunities for choral reading. Students read words and sentences together as you point to each word. Choral reading decreases MLs' anxiety about oral reading. Having students repeat after you is a good strategy when reading longer sentences.
- When teaching a language structure, place students in groups and have each group read a part of it aloud when cued by you. For example, when teaching *yesterday*, *today*, and *tomorrow* in connection with the days of the week, have one group read, "Yesterday was Sunday." The next group would read, "Today is Monday." The final group would read, "Tomorrow will be Tuesday." This activity can be repeated daily.

Grades 2–5

Reading in groups can be used for a variety of reading tasks at this stage including and beyond reading texts.

- If students are not yet ready to read independently, reading together will help them gain confidence. Give each student a copy of the same book, and have students take turns reading sections of text. Allow students to opt to just listen and follow along.
- Use choral reading when developing classroom rules or other anchor charts. Students can read the rules aloud as a class. Or place students in groups and have each group read one of the rules aloud. Each group can also create a poster with a visual depiction of the rule, which can then be posted in the classroom.
- At the start of the year, use choral reading regularly. For example, read instructions together as a class.

Grades 6–12

Use choral reading sparingly, as older students need greater accountability to participate. Group reading is effective for supporting students and ensuring participation.

- Assigning independent reading does not always ensure that MLs will read the material. Having students complete assigned reading in groups ensures MLs have access to the information, whether they are reading it aloud or listening to someone else read and following along.
- Determine groupings and divide text material thoughtfully to ensure each student can participate to the best of their ability. Groups can be mixed level (including a variety of language proficiency levels and native speakers of English) with the length of text determined in a way that allows higher-level students to read longer passages than lower-level students. Same-level groups can also be used to ensure you provide extra support to the lower-level groups.
- Assign students to read in pairs, alternating sentence by sentence.

More for You

Multilingual learners may have high affective filters, which hinder language acquisition. A high affective filter is the result of low confidence and high anxiety and stress when producing language. When the affective filter is high, students struggle with productive language. Choral reading as a group reduces students' anxiety and nervousness, lowering their affective filters.

Keep in Mind

Students who are still in the silent period of language acquisition need space to simply listen during group read-alouds. Choral reading is a low-risk opportunity for these students to participate if they choose.

Book Club

Engaging in discussion after reading helps students process what they read and retain more of the information. A book club format, with discussion questions that encourage students to summarize what they read, share their thoughts about the text, and ask questions, provides a less formal and more student-centered opportunity to process learning. Adjust book club requirements based on multilingual learners' language proficiency and reading levels to ensure they can participate without being overwhelmed. MLs also need a variety of access points. Always provide a reading guide, with questions students should answer as they read, to support multilingual students.

Make It Real

Grades PK–1

Book clubs in the early grades can focus on responding to a story that has been read aloud.

- After reading a story, retell it as a class, writing the sequence of events (what happened first, what happened next, and so on). Post the retelling in the classroom.
- As a class, illustrate a story. Have students draw the story; then post the drawings in the classroom. Students can draw one or two main events in the story, or even a depiction of the main character.
- Use these strategies during small-group reading to provide individual support.

Grades 2–5

Book clubs should help develop students' love of reading. Make book club fun, but also academically valuable.

- Provide books with access points for all reading levels. If you choose one book for the whole class to read, explore whether other versions are available, such a graphic novel version.
- Hold the book club once a week. Students read the assigned chapter(s) in advance. Use MLs' language acquisition level to determine the required amount of reading. Provide refreshments and seating choices. Engage in guided conversation about the book. Provide MLs with the questions in advance, so they can come prepared.

Grades 6–12

Book clubs can be used for novels and other literary reading, or for content-based instructional texts.

- Book club should provide students with the opportunity to review what they read, discuss the reading with their peers, and explore what they learned.
- Introduce the book club at the beginning of the semester. Create a structure that students will follow for meetings. The structure should include a schedule for reading the text, guided questions for discussion, and a final assignment based on the text students read.
- Make final assignments group endeavors with all members participating in the creation and presentation of the project.
- Ensure that at least one time during the semester the selected book is one students will enjoy reading for pleasure.

More for You

Provide students with several books to choose from for their book club. Place students into groups based on their book selection. Each group prepares a presentation about their book and presents it to the class.

Keep in Mind

Not all students are comfortable reading aloud. To lower students' affective filters, do not make reading out loud a requirement for participation in a book club. Additionally, it may be helpful to assign questions about the book to group members, so everyone can participate.

Pre-Write

Pre-writing is a strategy to support all students in their writing. For multilingual learners, pre-writing needs to be highly intentional. In addition to needing help developing and organizing their writing, MLs need every step of the pre-writing process scaffolded into small, attainable pieces. Expressly teach pre-writing (brainstorming, outlining, and organizing) and the writing process (structuring writing and using pre-writing to write drafts), breaking down each part into its individual components. For second grade and higher, provide guides for students to complete as they move through the writing process, with clear directions for each step of the guide.

Make It Real

Grades PK–1

Focus on the brainstorming element of pre-writing for these beginning writers.

- Model the process of thinking about what to write before starting to write. Using a picture or realia, brainstorm out loud all the parts of that item and then model figuring out how to write the words. For example, show an apple. Think out loud, "This is an apple. The apple is red. The apple is round." Then write those three words: *apple, red, round.*
- Repeat the process as a whole class during different topics of study. Show an item, then brainstorm all the things that describe the item. Write the words.
- Explain that brainstorming is important when writing. We have to think about what we want to write before we write it.

Grades 2–5

Expressly teach the pre-writing process and have students complete it for writing assignments.

- Teach students how to brainstorm, organize their brainstorm into a plan for their writing, and use the plan to write their assignment.
- MLs need more than a simple mind map. They need direct instruction and prompts for how to set up a brainstorm, what to include, and the structure to use. After brainstorming, take students through how to use the ideas generated to compose sentences. Follow this with how to group the sentences to develop paragraphs.
- Provide graphic organizers for each step of the pre-writing process and model how to complete them. Differentiate the organizers based on student needs. To support students with limited English language proficiency in developing productive language skills, provide partially completed organizers.

Grades 6–12

MLs in secondary grades are required to write increasingly complex assignments; the pre-writing process is critical for these students.

- Students at these levels need to be efficient when pre-writing. Summative assessments often need to be written quickly, which is an issue for MLs who require more time to complete writing tasks. Teach students how to complete short pre-writes that include the most important aspects, brainstorming and organizing their ideas prior to writing.
- Review students' pre-writes and final drafts to check their use of the process and to determine any re-teaching that needs to happen. Pre-writes provide insight into how MLs are progressing in vocabulary acquisition and their skills in transferring vocabulary into complete thoughts.

More for You

Once students become comfortable using pre-designed graphic organizers, have them start creating their own graphic organizers for brainstorming.

Keep in Mind

While students do not need to complete an entire pre-write for every writing assignment, they do need to be taught the benefits of brainstorming prior to writing in every subject area. Explain the importance of thinking through ideas before composing written drafts.

Focused Editing

Editing is challenging for multilingual learners who are writing in a new language. Explicitly teaching MLs what to look for will help them edit effectively. Provide guidelines that outline elements students should look for as they edit their own work and when peer editing. This needs to be more than a checklist; it should include examples. Adjust the guidelines as needed; students with lower-level English language proficiency should be looking for basics such as capital letters and periods, and the level of difficulty should increase as students' language skills develop.

Make It Real

Grades PK–1

Editing at these levels is similar whether students are MLs or native English speakers; they all are acquiring academic English.

- Teach students how to check for capital letters in proper names and at the start of sentences and end punctuation.
- Provide practice words and sentences that contain mistakes. Correct these as a class.
- After students have practiced, have them check their own writing for these elements.
- Students can practice editing single words, short phrases, and complete sentences, depending on their skill levels.

Grades 2–5

Help students with limited language proficiency build their editing skills.

- Begin with the basics for those new to learning English.
- Have students check for the elements of a paragraph—a topic sentence, details, and a closing sentence. Provide examples for students to reference.
- As students advance, have them look for specific elements, such as transition words.
- Place students in groups for peer editing. Assign each group member a specific element for which they are responsible.

Grades 6–12

Editing is more advanced as MLs are writing longer reports and exploring writing in various forms. MLs even at the earliest stages of language proficiency are expected to catch up quickly. Develop their skills throughout the semester.

- Incorporate and add to the elements covered in previous grades.
- Expand editing to include other forms of writing, such as writing for presentations.
- Provide an explicit checklist list of what students must address in their writing and include examples. Each student's work should be checked by at least two classmates.

Keep in Mind

It is critical to ensure MLs are able to edit their own work before allowing them to edit their peers' work. Be intentional when assigning roles for editing. Students need to actively participate and feel confident in their abilities; consider their English language proficiency levels and writing ability when giving them editing tasks.

Collaborative Writing

Writing in groups increases multilingual learners' confidence by sharing the risk and the responsibility for writing. Students develop writing skills as they work in collaboration to move through the writing process from brainstorming through writing a final draft. Prior to having students write in groups, engage in collaborative writing as a class, guiding every step of the process. Next, as students start writing in groups, scaffold the process by completing each step together as a class (e.g., discuss and model brainstorming, then have the students brainstorm together in their groups). Provide step-by-step instructions for the writing assignment and the process for collaborative writing. Post these instructions so students can refer to the steps as they work together. There are two parts that every group member participates in: choral reading and writing the paragraphs on their own papers.

Make It Real

Grades PK–1

Collaborative writing can be done as a whole class or in small groups with the teacher.

- Engage students in working together to write correct sentences. Ask a question such as, "What color is this apple?" and have students work together as a class to write the sentence. Students can then write the sentence on their own sheets of paper.
- Students do not have to physically write to collaborate on writing. For example, display a mixed-up sentence and work together to organize the parts of the sentence correctly.
- Have students brainstorm as a class. Give the group a topic, such as the weather, and guide students in collaborating to write as many words as they can think of that go with that topic.
- After brainstorming, help students create sentences about the topic using words they generated. Write the sentences on chart paper. Read the sentences aloud and have students repeat them.

Grades 2–5

Collaborative writing can be used as an introduction for different types of writing. Include a choral reading component to fully engage MLs in the final product.

- After teaching a form of writing and collaborating as a class on writing in that form, assign students to groups to practice.
- Divide the assignment into the steps of the writing process and give instructions for each step. Depending on the assignment, you may wish to plan for the steps to take place over several lessons.
- Use the writing process: brainstorm, pre-write (transferring the brainstorm into full ideas), first draft, edit, final draft. Explain each part and define students' roles during each part.
- When finished, have each group display and read their collaborative writing aloud to the class.

Grades 6–12

Students at these levels are working on academic knowledge as well as developing real-world skills, such as working in teams. Use collaborative writing for group projects and include a presentation component.

- Provide clear guidelines for group work. Ensure students know their individual roles/parts, and how they should differentiate their work to demonstrate they have completed their parts.
- Provide clear expectations for the project. Explain the steps the students will need to move through as they develop their final project.
- Provide a choices menu of products the groups may choose from for their final product (e.g., PowerPoint, written paper, performance, and so on). Include guidelines for each type of project.

More for You

Collaborative writing can be used to review content. Assign each group a different aspect of what was learned during the unit and have the groups write a paragraph on their topic; then read the paragraphs together as a class. Have students record these paragraphs and use them to study.

Keep in Mind

Knowing that productive language takes longer to acquire than receptive language, be intentional about group placement and assigned roles. Utilize students' language proficiency levels when making such decisions and identify ways that students with limited English language proficiency can meaningfully participate. Be explicit about which group members are responsible for which parts of the writing. One student can write the topic sentence, three students can each be responsible for a detail sentence, and the fourth student is responsible for the concluding sentence. You can also assign editing responsibilities. Use mechanisms to ensure each group member participates. For example, when students are writing on chart paper, give each student a colored marker to use for the parts they write.

Daily Writing

To improve writing fluency, multilingual learners should engage in daily writing practice. Journaling increases MLs' confidence in their writing, aids in vocabulary acquisition, and increases language and content retention. This can take the form of daily journal writing, responding to short prompts, or writing their thoughts about what they are learning. Daily writing should be a low-risk opportunity that is not highly structured. Provide a prompt and allow five to ten minutes for writing; the only requirement is that students write the whole time. You can provide a completion grade for daily writing, but it should not be assessed for technical elements, only for whether the student addressed the topic.

Make It Real

Grades PK–1

Practice writing letters and words or short sentences is effective at this level.

- Each day, have students respond to a simple writing prompt based on the instructional focus. For example, show a picture and have students write the words they think of when they see the picture, have students write all the days of the week, or have them write all the words they know for the weather. Base the writing task on students' abilities.
- Combine drawing and writing. Give students a phrase, such as "I like…" They copy the phrase and then finish it with a drawing of something they like. Students can write just one sentence or as many as they wish in the allotted time.

Grades 2–5

Daily writing can be content-specific but also fun, as the goal is writing fluency.

- Have students complete a daily journal responding to a prompt or writing from their own imaginations.
- At the close of the week, students turn in their journals. Journals are not graded, but it is beneficial to write something back to the students so they know you are reading their journals.
- Daily writing can also be used to review what students have learned. At the close of a lesson, have students write an "exit slip" about what they learned. This writing can be used for review later. Before the next lesson, students can write what they remember to jump-start their brains for engagement. This type of daily writing does not need to be in paragraphs or even sentences. Students can write lists or single words.

Continued

Grades 6–12

Use daily writing for students to process their learning and as a means for checking and connecting.

- Have students maintain journals that they complete at the end of class. The intention is for students to engage in conversation with you as their teacher. Students may reflect on their learning, write about anything they are thinking about, ask questions, or even write creatively.
- Check the journals once a week for completion. Rather than try to read all the journals every week, establish a rotating schedule to ensure you read and respond to each student's journal every few weeks.
- If a student needs a more immediate response because they have shared something important with you, they can put the journal on your desk to read that day.

More for You

Incorporate daily writing into lessons. Plan time at the close of a lesson or unit for students to summarize what they learned. Use composition books for daily summaries. This type of daily writing can be used in every subject area.

Keep in Mind

Daily writing does not have to be graded. If you choose to grade daily writing, the grade should not be based on length or on writing conventions. Base your expectations on each student's language proficiency level and writing ability. Use daily writing to identify students' strengths and areas where they may need additional instruction and support.

The Five Senses

Writing creatively as a multilingual learner can be difficult. Anchor writing to the five senses to give students direction when they are creating their own narratives. Using the five senses in writing provides students with support in writing independently, as they have a focus for their writing by describing what they or the character can see, smell, hear, taste, and touch.

Make It Real

Grades PK–1

Describing is a common aspect of learning in the early grades. The five senses are a natural fit for description.

- Connect the five senses to content topics. For example, when learning the seasons, as a class come up with five things you can see, smell, hear, taste, and touch during each of the seasons. Have students copy the words and draw pictures using the words as a guide.
- Explore the five senses to help students describe the experiences they have as they learn. For example, after students go outside for an activity, guide them through a discussion of what they could smell, see, hear, taste, and touch in their environment. Make a list as a class and have students copy the list.

Grades 2–5

Students in these grades are exploring new types of creative writing, including informational stories, personal narratives, and poetry. Use the five senses to help students practice each type of creative writing.

- Anchor creative writing assignments in the five senses. Provide the context for the story, poem, or personal narrative, and ask students to begin to brainstorm what they or a character might see, smell, hear, taste, or touch in that context. Students can start with a single paragraph or stanza that incorporates all five of the senses. As they become more skilled in writing, have them write a paragraph or stanza for each sense.
- During field trips, have students take note of what they see, smell, hear, taste, and touch. When students return to the classroom, have them each write a narrative of their experience.

Continued

Grades 6–12

Creative writing can be used in multiple content areas. Students can create character sketches, explore a period in history, or examine the natural world. The five senses are concrete elements that can add depth to students' writing.

- Use the five senses as a jumping-off point for students. When writing creatively, getting started can be the hardest part. Have students start with these concrete elements.
- When writing longer pieces, whether fiction, informational, personal narrative, or poetry, have students incorporate the five senses in each new scene or part.
- Personal narratives are a good means through which to connect students with content and tap into prior experience and knowledge. Anchor these narratives in the five senses to provide a concrete base for students to work from.

More for You

Try this strategy with comic strips. Have students create short comic strips to tell a story or an experience. Require that five of the comic strip blocks focus on the five senses.

Keep in Mind

Concrete language is easier for MLs to acquire than abstract language. The five senses help students use concrete language that is accessible within their environments. As students make progress in their language acquisition, have them add abstract ideas or memories in connection with the concrete elements they see, smell, hear, taste, and touch to provide more challenge. For example, meat cooked on the stove tasted like the smoky air in summer, or the sweet cinnamon in the tea felt like a warm sweater on a cold day.

Navigating Instructional Texts

Textbooks contain rich information beyond their main text. There are illustrations, graphs, tables, and other features students must know how to read. Intentionally teach students how to access all the information in instructional texts. Any time a new text is introduced, take students through its features and components. Think critically about the information that is most useful for students and teach those elements first. It is important not to overwhelm multilingual learners. One way to support them is to provide a guide to the specific text elements they should use.

Make It Real

Grades PK–1

At these levels, students may be using consumable texts.

- Each time you give MLs new consumable texts, take a book tour. If possible, do this in small groups.
- Beginning with the front cover, read the title. Guide students in describing what the title and illustration tell them about what to expect inside the book.
- Take MLs through the first couple of activities in the consumable text. Identify the header items, usually name and date. Then explore the page. Where are the directions, and how should students look for the important information?
- Discuss the structure of a page and how to follow the flow, left to right and top to bottom.

Grades 2–5

Explicitly teach MLs to navigate the texts for different subject areas.

- Before assigning reading or activities in a text, teach MLs how to use it. Take them through a chapter, looking at elements such as the title, headings, images, illustrations, and so on. Discuss the information each feature provides.
- Review features such as a glossary and appendix. Explain the purpose of each feature and how to use it.
- Give an assignment that asks students to navigate the text to find certain features and information. You may wish to pair MLs with English-speaking partners. Or have them work in high-low language proficiency pairings. Monitor the pairs to ensure lower-level MLs are participating and understanding.

Grades 6–12

MLs need explicit instructions in navigating the complex textbooks found at these levels.

- Teach MLs how to read charts and graphs. Guide students in navigating the headers, labels, legends, axes, and so on. Explain how charts and graphs are laid out and how to read them. Provide students with practice in reading these features.
- When first asking MLs to read a chapter in a textbook, provide a guide for them to follow, directing students to specific elements in the chapter. Have students take notes based on this guide. After students have used the guide successfully, gradually expect them to be more independent in locating information on their own.

More for You

Students often skip over directions when working in a consumable text or answering comprehension and review questions at the end of a chapter. Explain the importance of reading and following the directions, and teach students how to do so efficiently by looking for important words and phrases.

Keep in Mind

Not all languages are read from left to right and top to bottom. Be clear with students the direction they should follow when navigating a page, not only that the eyes should move across the page from left to right and down the page from top to bottom, but also how to efficiently scan a page for key information—titles, headings, illustrations, charts, or graphs—and then read the main text.

Examining Visuals

Visual literacy is essential to learning a new language, as students must navigate visuals to support their language learning. Multilingual learners benefit from practice describing, analyzing, and interpreting the elements of visuals, such as colors and shapes, especially because visuals are used to illustrate or support English language text. Visuals often enhance or expand the meaning of fictional and informational books, instructional texts, and classroom materials such as anchor charts. Learning to analyze visuals helps develop critical thinking skills, which translates into analysis in the other domains of language.

Make It Real

Grades PK–1

- Have students compare images to find differences and similarities. For example, they can compare how illustrations show a character's changing emotions.
- When reading aloud, help students look for clues in the illustrations. Ask questions that engage students in making inferences about emotions, relationships, and so on.
- Teach students the meaning of visual cues such as exit signs, arrows, and sign shapes (e.g., the octagonal shape of a stop sign).

Grades 2–5

- Have a scavenger hunt. Provide a topic and have students find or create visuals that connect to that topic.
- Have students compare visuals to find similarities and differences. Then have students write about the similarities and differences.
- Use visuals such as emojis to help MLs discuss how they are feeling or to process an experience. Students can also create visuals to communicate during difficult conversations.

Grades 6–12

- Visual analysis is appropriate for artistic works, science-related images, math models, primary sources in social studies, and more.
- Provide a visual and have students work in groups to discuss their ideas about its meaning.
- After students process their thinking, have them write what they believe the visual means, what they learn from it, how it relates to the content, what emotions it evokes, what the artist is trying to say, and so on.
- Explicitly teach how symbolism is used in visuals.

More for You

Have students create visual representations of the learning in a lesson or unit. Display the visuals in the classroom and have students explain their images. Use the visuals for review.

Keep in Mind

Described as the fifth language domain, visual literacy is about communication and interpretation. Just as students need to learn to read, write, listen, and speak, they also need to understand how to interpret, communicate about, and communicate using visuals.

Visual Projects

Visual projects provide opportunities for students to practice and demonstrate visual literacy. Students can create posters, graphics, or digital presentations to accompany written and oral assignments or as stand-alone projects. Creating visual projects is an opportunity for multilingual learners to demonstrate their learning through visual outputs, which in turn supports their skills in interpreting visuals. Additionally, visual products are a way to differentiate assessment. Multilingual learners with lower English language proficiency can demonstrate understanding through visual representations instead of through writing or speaking.

Make It Real

Grades PK–1

Help young students create simple projects that demonstrate their learning.

- Any topic can translate into a summative visual project. For example, when learning about habitats, students could create posters showing features of a habitat. Help students label their creations.
- Engage students in completing a visual project about content from a unit. For example, students could create a visual booklet about healthful foods. Support students in writing short sentences for each page.

Grades 2–5

Guide students in articulating how their project represents their learning.

- Have students work in groups and assign each group a different section of a unit. Each group creates a collage incorporating content they learned. Display the collages to review the entire unit.
- Have students create visuals that represent feelings based on a specific experience. For example, have students create visuals that represent their feelings just before the start of the school year.

Grades 6–12

Visual projects are engaging, and they provide a break from writing reports or developing oral presentations.

- Creating visuals is a good alternative to traditional homework. Have students make posters, drawings, or displays to review or demonstrate understanding.
- At the close of a unit, have students create a visual book about what they learned. Allow students to use any style they choose—picture book, graphic novel, and so on.

More for You

To build community, create a mural. Have students create images that represent who they are, their interests, and so on. Ensure each image is the same size. Post them as a mural on the classroom wall.

Keep in Mind

Ensure that students understand the expectations by providing a rubric. For example, for a final project on photosynthesis and its effect, assessment would be based on accurate inclusion of each step in the process and whether the visual clearly represents the effect of photosynthesis on the planet.

Leveled Assessment

One of the most important means through which to accommodate students' language proficiency levels is through assessment. Adjust assessments through structured support and by allowing students to demonstrate their understanding in multiple ways. When constructing assessment questions, eliminate information that may distract students from the actual question. The goal is for students to demonstrate understanding of the content, not wade through complicated questions. Ensure that what you are asking of students is clear.

Make It Real

Grades PK–1

Pictures and oral response are good options for assessment.

- Ask students to demonstrate what they know through drawing. Give them a prompt and ask them to draw what they heard or the answer to the question.
- Total physical response is an effective form of formative assessment. Vocabulary such as verbs can be acted out, along with other content that can be expressed through movement.
- One-to-one conversations are useful in the early grades.
- Have children point or gesture to classify or sort items shown on picture cards. This can be done using a whiteboard or a T-chart made of tape on a table.

Grades 2–5

Content becomes more complex and formal assessments are a necessity in the middle elementary grades.

- Provide scaffolded assessments based on how much support students need for completing them. For example, students at proficiency level 1 and still in the receptive or early production phase can draw responses to short-answer questions or give one-to-two-word responses.
- Use word economy when writing directions. Use only the language that is necessary for students to understand what they need to do. Instead of a paragraph, write a list or limit the number of sentences in the instructions to one or two. For example: *Write an "I am" poem. 1. Complete the sentences with information about you. 2. Add a picture of you. The picture can be a drawing or a photo.*

Continued

Grades 6–12

Instruction moves quickly in secondary grades. Leveled assessment is critical to ensure students are keeping pace.

- For written assessments such as document-based questions, provide scaffolded options for students based on their language levels and productive abilities.
- Grade students based on the content details they provide. For example, for students at level 1, provide a fully scaffolded option, with sentence frames, transition words, and hints as to the data expectations. For level 2 and 3 students, provide sentence starters only, and for level 4 students, use the original assessment.
- Allow students to demonstrate understanding via several modalities, e.g., visual representations, performances, or talking about what they know.

More for You

Consider allowing students to complete assessments in their preferred language if you are fluent in the language or can grade the assessment via an interpreter or translation service. Ensure students are literate in their preferred language before offering this option. This information is sometimes available in a students' file via transcripts or an assessment test for biliteracy. Or you may be able to discuss this during parent-teacher conferences.

Keep in Mind

Regardless of English language proficiency level, students must have access to the same instruction and content as their peers who are native speakers of English. Accommodation rather than modification is critical when addressing the needs of MLs.

Oral Assessments

Oral assessments offer teachers an opportunity to connect with students one-to-one, check in, and assess where students are with their learning. Providing an oral component to assessments also adds one more way through which students can demonstrate their learning, making assessment more accessible for students at all language proficiency levels. Use a clear rubric as you give an oral assessment. Try to keep the assessment as similar as possible for different students. It is acceptable to rephrase or ask additional questions to elicit a correct response, but follow the same general protocol for every student.

Make It Real

Grades PK–1

- Focus on using vocabulary correctly in context. Show pictures and have students say the vocabulary they know based on the picture.
- Engage in basic conversation with students based on the content. For example, if working on introductions, introduce yourself to the student and have them respond.
- Check in to see how students are doing and ask questions that will help you get to know them better.
- Have a clear rubric to use as a basis for recording the results of the oral assessment.

Grades 2–5

- Oral assessments should focus on the target language for the unit. This can be a conversation you have with a student. Assess word choice, phrasing, and clarity of message. Look for a natural flow of conversation rather than highly specific wording.
- During the oral assessment, ask students questions about how they are feeling in class, if they need additional support, and their interests, likes, dislikes, and so on, to get to know them better.

Grades 6–12

- Ask content-specific questions. Elicit similar information in both oral assessments and written assessments. This will allow students multiple ways to demonstrate their understanding.
- In addition to adding an oral component to summative assessments, include an oral component to unit assessments. Oral assessments can help you determine if reteaching is needed prior to moving on.
- Use the time to check in, get to know students better, and find out what additional supports they need.

More for You

Many English language development curriculums provide an oral assessment at the end of each unit. The assessment is usually a speaking test. Expand the speaking test to assess content comprehension as well.

Keep in Mind

Oral assessments can be used for formative and summative assessments. Because oral assessments are one-to-one, they provide an opportunity to connect with and assess each individual student, and they are lower risk for students, as students are not required to speak in front of their peers.

Targeted Self-Assessment

Self-assessment is an essential skill for every student. Multilingual learners need guided support to ensure self-assessment is meaningful. Provide students with structures through which they can complete self-assessments that help them be more independent learners. Multilingual learners need a guide with targeted questions they understand and can answer about their work. When using self-assessments with MLs, it is critical to complete the first several self-assessments with them to help them learn from what they observe in their own work and use that information to improve it prior to turning it in.

Make It Real

Grades PK–1

- Have students self-assess by responding to questions or statements about their learning. Display responses, such as *yes*, *almost*, *not yet*. Have students select responses, providing help as needed. For example, the self-assessment might include a statement such as, "I know the parts of a plant." The student would name the parts and, depending on their knowledge, choose *yes*, *almost*, or *not yet*.
- To check for understanding, have students complete quick self-assessments using hand gestures. For example, ask the class to show a thumbs up, thumbs to the side, or thumbs down in response to the statement, "In this set of numbers, I know which number is the largest." This is a quick way to determine if reteaching is necessary for all or some of the class.

Grades 2–5

Self-assessment is an essential part of having a growth mindset and participating in learning.

- Provide students with a checklist to use to assess their work. This can be a simple list that they use to determine what elements they have completed or still need to complete.
- Have a list of questions students can use to self-assess periodically. Take time to pause during lessons and have students ask these questions of themselves. Check in to see if students need additional support based on the questions.
- Use hand signals like those described for grades PK–1 for quick checks for understanding.

Grades 6–12

Self-assessment is critical at the secondary level to give students agency in a high stakes-environment.

- Provide rubrics to students to use to assess their work prior to turning it in for a grade. The rubrics should be clear and without any unnecessary verbiage. Provide space on the rubrics for students to record what they did or understood completely and what they still need to learn or work on. Use the same rubrics to complete your assessment of student work.
- At the close of lessons, have students write summaries of their learning along with assessments of how well they feel they understood the lesson. Have them write at least one question they have about the content.
- Use hand signals for quick checks.

More for You

Students can work together to complete self-assessments. Have students ask one another guided questions about the lesson, assignment, or project. Through this discussion, students can assess their learning or performance/work.

Keep in Mind

For self-assessment to be meaningful, students must have full understanding of the purpose of the assignment, project, or lesson, and the expectations for their learning and work products. The first priority when teaching content or assigning work is to ensure students understand what they are supposed to learn and do, and why.

Targeted Feedback

Multilingual learners need individualized and targeted feedback, with an emphasis on use and mastery of content language. A uniform rubric for grading and feedback can be beneficial in guiding assessment, but rubrics need to be tailored to address language and student needs. Rubrics also need to be adjusted for clarity to ensure they are accessible for MLs. The rubric should be easily navigated, with language that is simple and clear. Focus on the content and on language elements such as grammar, pronunciation, vocabulary usage, and writing structures (depending on the assignment). Provide specific and constructive feedback orally and in writing to ensure MLs know what they did well and what they need to work on. Keep the feedback constructive rather than overly critical to avoid increasing the student's affective filter, making them reluctant to produce language.

Make It Real

Grades PK–1

Use oral feedback with young learners.

- Ensure feedback is specific and easy to understand. When MLs make speaking errors, repeat the sentence or phrase correctly and have them repeat after you.
- Be positive. Positive reinforcement is essential as students are developing a love of learning and learning to take risks in producing language.
- Ensure feedback is specific. Instead of saying, "Good job," tell students specifically what they did well.
- Choose one or two mistakes students made during a lesson. Without naming the students, correct these as a class. Students will know if they made the mistake but will not feel targeted.

Grades 2–5

Students in these grades are beginning to get written feedback.

- Instead of simply marking test answers incorrect, specify the correct answer.
- When language mistakes are made, in addition to marking the mistake, write out the language correctly so students can see it.
- Have students review their tests to learn from them. In the beginning, review tests with students. Focus on the questions that were missed by multiple students. Provide language practice opportunities for repeated errors.
- When responding to MLs' writing, be specific about what they did well and what they need to work on, focusing on language structures and correct use of vocabulary.
- Make sure students understand the reasons for scores they receive. Grades need to be meaningful, and students need to know how to grow from their mistakes.

Grades 6–12

Because of the higher stakes in secondary grades, students should be provided opportunities to redo their work based on feedback.

- Use the same rubric for grading as you provide to MLs for their assignment.
- Explain why students scored as they did on the rubric and give them an opportunity to redo the assignment at least once based on feedback.
- Provide positive and constructive feedback. Students at the secondary level still need positive reinforcement, especially MLs with high affective filters. Without positive reinforcement, they will be reluctant to produce language. Students need to know where they succeeded in addition to where they need improvement.
- Provide two feedback elements for MLs for every assignment—content-specific feedback and language-specific feedback.

More for You

It is better to model than to correct. Instead of telling a student they phrased something incorrectly, repeat what they said using correct phrasing. Do this as often as necessary.

Keep in Mind

It is critical to know your students' language proficiency levels. Understanding their language proficiency levels will help you understand what to expect of them in terms of receptive and productive language. Use these levels to provide feedback that will help them progress to the next level of proficiency.

References

Asher, James. 2009. *Learning Another Language Through Actions,* 7th edition. Los Gatos, CA: Sky Oaks Productions.

¡Colorín Colorado!. n.d. "Project-Based Learning for ELLs." Accessed February 13, 2024. colorincolorado.org/ell/pbl.

Cummins, Jim. 2008. "BICS and CALP: Empirical and Theoretical Status of the Distinction." In *Encyclopedia of Language and Education, Volume 2: Literacy, 2nd edition*, edited by Brian Street and Nancy H. Hornberger, 71–83. New York: Springer Science + Business Media LLC.

El Yaafouri, Louise. 2017. "How Home Visits Transformed My Teaching." *Educational Leadership* 75 (1): 20–25. ascd.org/el/articles/how-home-visits-transformed-my-teaching/.

Fisher, Douglas, and Nancy Frey. 2010. "Unpacking the Language Purpose: Vocabulary, Structure, and Function." *TESOL Journal* 1 (3): 315–337. doi.org/10.5054/tj.2010.227607.

FluentU. 2023. "7 Must-Use Types of Visual Aids in Teaching English." *FluentU English Educator Blog*. September 15, 2023. fluentu.com/blog/educator-english/esl-visual-aids/#toc_7.

Frey, Nancy, and Douglas Fisher. 2011. *The Formative Assessment Action Plan: Practical Steps to More Successful Teaching and Learning*. Alexandria, VA: ASCD.

Haiken, Michele. 2021. "5 Ways to Gamify Your Classroom." *ISTE Learning Library*. February 12, 2021. iste.org/blog/5-ways-to-gamify-your-classroom.

Kelley, Shannon. n.d. "Retelling: An Evidence-Based Literacy Strategy." *Understood*. Accessed February 13, 2024. understood.org/en/articles/how-to-teach-retelling.

Krashen, Stephen D. 1981. *Second Language Acquisition and Second Language Learning*. Oxford: Pergamon.

Krashen, Stephen D., and Tracey D. Terrell. 1983. *The Natural Approach: Language Acquisition in the Classroom*. San Francisco: Alemany.

Let's TEACH. 2016. "Instructional Strategies—The Ten Plus Two Teaching Method." January 24, 2016, YouTube, 0:31. youtube.com/watch?v=Y2udPWz_3vg/.

Link, Laura J., and Thomas R. Guskey. 2022. "Is Standards-Based Grading Effective?" *Theory Into Practice* 61 (4): 406–417. doi.org/10.1080/00405841.2022.2107338.

Robertson, Kristina, and Karen Ford. n.d. "Language Acquisition: An Overview." *¡Colorín Colorado!*. Accessed February 13, 2024. colorincolorado.org/article/language-acquisition-overview/.

Shapiro, Shawna. 2022. *Cultivating Critical Language Awareness in the Writing Classroom*. New York: Routledge.

Swain, Merrill. 2005. "The Output Hypothesis: Theory and Research." In *Handbook of Research in Second Language Teaching and Learning*, edited by Eli Hinkel, 471–483. London: Routledge.

WIDA. 2007. *The WIDA English Language Proficiency Standards, PreKindergarten through Grade 12*. Board of Regents of the University of Wisconsin System.

WIDA. 2020. *WIDA English Language Development Standards Framework, 2020 Edition: Kindergarten–Grade 12*. Board of Regents of the University of Wisconsin System.

Wolpert-Gawron, Heather. 2018. "PBL with English Language Learners: A Vital Need." *PBLWorks*. June 13, 2018. pblworks.org/blog/pbl-english-language-learners-vital-need.

Zelazo, Philip David, Clancy B. Blair, and Michael T. Willoughby. 2016. "Executive Function: Implications for Education." (NCER 2017-2000) Washington, DC: National Center for Education Research, Institute of Education Sciences, U.S. Department of Education.

